VIRTUAL EDUCATION AND EDUCATIONAL FUTURES

VIRTUAL EDUCATION AND EDUCATIONAL FUTURES

Editor
Prof. Ramesh Chandra

Publications
KALPAZ PUBLICATIONS
DELHI-110052

VIRTUAL EDUCATION AND EDUCATIONAL FUTURES

Virtual Education and Educational Futures

Rs. 870

ISBN: 81-7835-238-9

This book is Vol. No. 10 of Universal Education and Technology in 21st Century (Set)

Published in 2005 in India by
Kalpaz Publications,
C-30, Satyawati Nagar, Delhi-110052
E-mail : Kalpaz@hotmail.com

Laser Typesetting at : Master Computers, Delhi
Printed at : Ajit Printers, Delhi

Contents

Preface

The new information and communication technologies transformed the concepts of educational system we have followed traditionally. Now we are the netizens of the virtual millennium where the advent of virtual classrooms and video-desktop technologies promises interesting possibilities of teaching and learning at anyplace, anytime and anywhere. With the improvement in network capabilities and course content, online education is becoming a viable alternative to taking courses in the classroom. Not only does online education provide a relative price advantage but it also provides a wide range of course materials. Coursework offerings range from professional growth to on-the-job training.

Virtual learning environments represent an entirely new form of educational technology. They offer the educational institutions of the world a complex set of opportunities and challenges. An example of a virtual learning environment is a package, which supports learners as they work with mathematical formulae and makes it possible for them while using the package to send mathematical working, tables of values and mathematical sketches to other students and tutors, and to receive similar information back from them, either while they are working or later. It is the combination of individualised adaptive interaction with communication on demand that provides the unique form of support for the learner.

Virtual education allows users to learn information from any location that has internet access. It offers numerous benefits to individuals, organisations, and even to society in general. For individuals, it provides access to education or training that they may not otherwise be able to pursue. For organisations it provides a cost efficient way to train or educate a large number of learners irrespective of their geographical location. As individuals are offered more opportunities to learn, distance learning might end up being an avenue to increase the overall literacy in society through greater access to education.

Editor

1

Virtual Learning Environments

Virtual learning environments represent an entirely new form of educational technology. They offer the educational institutions of the world a complex set of opportunities and challenges. An example of a virtual learning environment is a package, which supports learners as they work with mathematical formulae and makes it possible for them while using the package to send mathematical working, tables of values and mathematical sketches to other students and tutors, and to receive similar information back from them, either while they are working or later. It is the combination of individualised adaptive interaction with communication on demand that provides the unique form of support for the learner. A classroom or a library is an example of a real learning environment, and a computer program which supports a non-trivial scientific simulation can be considered to be an interactive learning environment.

A virtual learning environment may support similar forms of learning to a 'real' one but it is not a physical space like a classroom or lecture. In addition to having a different relation to space and time, a virtual learning environment will also be different from a real one with respect to memory. Virtual learning environments are realised with computer technology, and can thus be designed to have their own memory of what the learner or group of learners have been doing. Virtual learning environments are a relatively recent development and they arise from the convergence of computer and communication technologies that has accelerated over the last ten years.

The educational community has only recently begun to think through the possibilities for learning environments that are not restricted to particular places and times and that can remember past events. But associated with the possibilities are some very serious challenges and concerns. For any particular virtual learning environment we need to identify the types of human teaching role that are necessary to support learning gains, and how the number of persons in the teaching role changes as the number of learners rises.

Some virtual learning environments can yield significant economies of scale and provide a route for enhancing educational provision in countries where educational resources are very limited. Others do not yield economies of scale, and in fact require extra layers of human administrative support as student numbers rise.

In helping to reconfigure how learners can learn, modern information and communications technology presents a very complex set of challenges for teachers and teaching. There are nearly 60 million teachers in the world's formal education systems alone. Up to now, the implications of recent developments in information and communications technology for teachers and teaching have probably not received the attention at the international level that they merit. The traditional mode of contact between teacher and learner, at least that on which the world's formal education systems have been largely constructed, has been face to face in the classroom.

Modern information and communications technology challenges the traditional teacher-class relationship, in particular the necessity for face to face contact. The design of virtual learning environments is surely a pedagogical or teaching activity. We are beginning to witness, it seems, the emergence of a new class of teachers: people who are never seen at all, even at a distance, by learners, yet who essentially determine how learners are going to go about their learning tasks.

Evolution of educational technology

Educational technology was an important concern in the latter part of the last century as attempts were made in Europe and the United States to implement effective systems of universal schooling. Vannevar Bush, through his MEMEX machine, proposed a method of cataloguing and retrieving information based on associations rather than on hierarchical systems when one item is within its grasp it snaps instantly to the next that is suggested by association of thoughts in accordance with some intricate web of trails carried by the cells of the brain.

Engelbart (the designer of the mouse and 'father' of e-mail) further developed this concept producing, in 1960, his system AUGMENT which stored information in ways which allowed non-hierarchical browsing accessed by the mouse, and with viewing filters to improve efficiency. However it was Nelson who coined the term Hypertext to mean non-sequential writing and his publishing system XANADU linked electronic documents and other media such as audio and graphics. Thus Hypermedia came into being, but note that initially these systems were self-contained and used specific equipment.

The development of the Internet, form its military origins to a world-wide client-server computing network with a common protocol, was followed by the establishment of the World Wide Web in Geneva. Hypertext documents that could incorporate multimedia materials, and followed specified 'mark-up' conventions known as HTML (Hypertext Mark-up Language), were able to be placed on the Internet thus forming a distributed interconnected library of documents. Through these common protocols and conventions, users were able to produce and access materials and did not need to concern themselves with the particulars of individual computing systems.

Hence the prospect of having a Virtual World-wide Library of Material - produced by a population of potential users who could communicate and engage in collaborative projects (the initial impetus for the development of World Wide Web) - became a practical reality.

For knowledge acquisition, developments in Hypermedia and the Internet/World Wide Web provide a network of content, but raise problems of learning management and control. Structuring by function, adaptive navigation and related open-access question asking/answering can provide support. For knowledge application, multimedia simulations and virtual reality scenarios increase interactivity and the scope of learning with broadband networks enabling Videoconferencing to be a learning support.

Collaborative study methods using conferencing techniques have been developed, but how are all these resources and techniques to be organised effectively into distributed learning systems ? Some use the conventional curriculum as a focus, but other developments are less constrained and aim for greater multi-user interactivity and sense of presence. They use a wider range of organisational metaphors, and place tools for organising learning with teachers and students.'

Although the main drivers for the development of virtual learning environments are technological, developments in cognitive science, instructional theory and ideas of educational reform also have a role. A synoptic review of cognitively-oriented initiatives for reform in education which is diverse both in form and in theory. Most, however, can be clustered together around a small set of underlying themes. Three such themes are

i) Activeness,

ii) Collegiality, and

iii) Authenticity.

One important goal of current reform is to effect a shift in the student's role from one of passivity to one that necessitates active engagement in the learning process, that is to increase student Activeness. This has been an a recurrent theme in educational reform efforts in this country for many years. Past innovations in instructional practice designed to increase Activeness include "learning by discovery", open-classroom learning, experiential learning, and inquiry learning.

Congruent with this movement to increase learner Activeness, another focus of change has been toward increased Collegiality in the teacher's role within the classroom. Traditionally, the teacher's role has been to "acquire formal knowledge, find efficient ways of sharing it, and determine whether pupils have learned what was taught". Reform efforts, however, have attempted to transform this traditional role into one of team facilitator or learning coach. Research in the emerging area of Computer Supported Collaborative Learning has focused on the ways that technology might be used to support reform on the dimension of Collegiality.

A third theme for instructional reform has been to dissolve the barriers between what one does and studies within the confines of school and the aptitudes called for in the world outside of school, that is, to increase the Authenticity of the curriculum through the design of new instructional materials and curricula. Theoretical approaches, such as Situated Cognition, call for increasing the resemblance between contexts of learning and contexts of application.

Technology can, and has been, used in a variety of ways to support authenticity in instruction. It can, for example, increase the realism with which problems are presented to learners, or facilitate the storage and retrieval of instructive cases . Technology can also support Authenticity by providing a window onto the world outside of the classroom while at the same time, helping to make the activities of the classroom more visible to the surrounding community.

Each of these three themes can be seen as orthogonal to the other two in that each addresses a different aspect of reform. Activeness, for example, concerns changes in the role of the learner, while Collegiality is more concerned with changes in the traditional role of the teacher. Authenticity, on the other hand, is concerned with the design of new curricular structures and the materials needed to support such curricula.

There is currently a wide range of technological choices with respect to both communication and computer technologies, and each instance of a virtual learning environment can be viewed as essentially based on a pair of choices which must together support some category of learners in some physical setting.

Over the last decade, a research team at New Jersey Institute of Technology has been involved in constructing a specific version which we called the Virtual Classroom, and studying its use in a wide variety of courses, including all of the major courses for a BA in Information Systems degree.' These take advantage of the combination of electronic mail packages augmented to support computer conferences with the types of communication networks found within technologically advanced educational institutions.

While there are many questions regarding the quality and value of what is learned from television, there is no question that television is a widespread, visual, virtual, and powerful learning environment. In the Middle East, the number of households that have televisions is estimated to be 50 million. In India cable television access scales up in leaps of millions, as well. The success of television in developing countries shows an acceptance rate similar to what has been experienced in North America.

People everywhere accept, like, and enjoy television. But behind the success of television, as an information medium, lies a very powerful concept for network infrastructure: the broadcast mode. Deployed as a broadcast infrastructure for the dissemination of information, "television" can be leveraged to address the serious problem of global education. But, its effectiveness has been limited by the number of educational approaches that could be deployed, until now mostly analogue broadcasts and live video over satellite.

Taking advantage of new opportunities offered by Digital Broadcast Satellite, a new global education infrastructure can involve the teacher much more and in critical roles. A new broadcast system (for equity access) coupled with a complementary information organisation model and guided in its use (for content convergence) can become a powerful and efficient, universal and global educational fore, that can be deployed at moderate cost, and can reach remote locations with or without coupling with the Internet. This system can provide true equity access and quality.

Technological Trends

Education exerts a weak 'pull' on the development of computer and communication technologies and for the most part, like many other important areas of human activity, is subject to the 'push' of new quite general products intended for the world marketplace. The last forty years have seen a steady exponential reduction in the cost of manufacturing both computer memory and computer processors. This has now resulted in the availability of powerful 'personal' computers linked by networks to 'server' computers holding data and programs associated with different enterprises.

A key aspect of the contemporary personal computer is the graphical user interface which makes it possible for the user to control many aspects of the computer's functions by pointing at pictures rather than by typing instructions. The educational institutions of some countries are relatively computer rich and some schools now have a computer in every classroom, or classrooms in which for a number of hours a week pupils may have individual use of a networked personal computer. In other countries pupils or even teachers will not encounter computers as part of routine schooling. Both between countries and within countries access to computer technology is very heterogeneous, but the long-term tendency will continue to be greater access to powerful computers designed for individual use.

For educationalists it is important to recognise that modern computers with their keyboards, small screen and pointing devices such as mice have evolved into personal media which for the user are similar to books and notepads and quite different from blackboards and lectures. At the same time it is becoming easier to work with others via personal computers, because the additional technological push associated with this decade is the increasing integration of computer and communication technologies. This integration manifests itself in various ways with a key historical distinction between asynchronous modes and synchronous modes of learning and working.

Asynchronous modes include electronic mail, computer conferencing, access to remote databases and to the World Wide Web. In these modes the provider of information knows that there is an audience for which they are preparing information. This may be an individual learner, a class or anyone with interest and

Internet access who will read and perhaps react to the information provided at some unspecified future time.

Synchronous modes include digital broadcasting, screen sharing, on-line blackboards, video links and audio links. In these modes, the learners and teachers can respond to each other in real time, selecting and storing information for future use or making changes to a running computer simulation whose consequences are immediately apparent to the other active learners and teachers.

We can predict an integration of tools used by learners for sending messages and sharing running simulations with the tools for authoring materials and for browsing databases and World Wide Web pages. Such integration is highly desirable for ease of use and without it there is a real risk that the proliferation of new digital information sources will create an unmanageable burden for teachers and learners.

The three critical aspects are the integration of information and communication technologies, the integration of synchronous and asynchronous modes of use and the integration of tools for search and construction of digital learning materials. Such integration could make networks much more transparent and the Internet as easy to use as the telephone, especially as computer input devices become even simpler and support pointing and speech rather than requiring the typing of strings of colons, dots and slashes.

The educational systems around the world are subject to resource pressures of varying degree and in many parts of the world there is limited access to physical networks that can support reliable high speed digital communication. So the cost of the technology is critical. We can now predict with some confidence the eventual possibility of small robust wireless networked personal computers that are relatively cheap to manufacture and that have the additional functionality of a telephone, television, fax, etc.

But the way the ubiquitous computer of the future will be marketed is much harder to predict. Given the past behaviour of the leading companies and the fact that there can be commercial benefits associated with incompatible hardware, software and communication standards it is necessary to be very cautious about the timing of universal world educational access to the technologies that are needed to support virtual learning environments.

Pedagogical Approaches

Educational research laboratories that specialise in this area are supported by manufacturers who provide prototype hardware and software in exchange for glimpses of possible future applications of their new technologies in schools and colleges.

A variety of reasons are given to encourage the use of computers to support student learning. In this account we focus on those reasons that are based on the unique properties that computers have:

— the simulation capability, so that students can watch, for example, computer animations of dangerous nuclear reactions;
— the communication and database capability enabling students to have quick access to information;

— the input and output devices which make it possible for disabled students with little movement to control computers and for blind students to hear spoken computer output;

— the re-programmability which makes it possible in principle to improve steadily and systematically existing learning materials.

— the ability to interact adaptively with individual students;

— the patient, instant feedback and tolerance for error.

An engineering approach akin to that used in work in artificial intelligence or computer human interaction is usually taken. Researchers stress the value of formative evaluation, collecting both numerical information and qualitative data such as protocols of learner use of the innovative system.

The researchers tend to work in multi-disciplinary teams, adopting in part or whole the ethnomethodological approaches associated with anthropologists and searching for good quality longitudinal data. They often target particularly needy or deserving communities of learners for their pioneering experiments and are always concerned with addressing the Hawthorne effect whereby learning gains might be induced by the motivation associated with novelty rather than any inherent educational quality of the innovation.

To the extent that the researchers in this area adopt theoretical positions these tend to influence the set of research questions worked on rather than directly inform the design of the virtual learning environments. The majority of researchers adopt a neo-Piagetian constructivist approach. They take a strongly cognitive view of learning tempered by a strong concern with how groups of learners construct knowledge together in social situations.

Associated with this line are concerns with reciprocal tutoring, with the cultural setting in which the learning is taking place and the drivers for change in learner motivation. There is a natural affinity with some of the concerns of cognitive science particularly the difficult notion of distributed cognition.

Cognition can be viewed as distributed in some community of learners and distributed in an individual who may have multiple and partial understandings of the same concepts or processes. This then adds to the research agenda the questions of how to link procedural and conceptual knowledge, the role of external representation in cognition and identifying the psychological processes integral to deep conceptual learning.

Properties of Virtual Learning Environments

It is important to identify the ways that these new learning media are qualitatively different from other types of learning material. The special properties of computers can used to enhance student learning processes on a number of orthogonal dimensions.

Visualisation

By augmenting simulation engines, symbolic calculators and other software with graphical output it becomes possible to support student visualisation of highly abstract processes and procedures.

Diagnosis

By tracking student work on related tasks it becomes possible to distinguish 'accidental' errors from those which provide statistical evidence for failure to understand key concepts or to master critical skills.

Remediation

By systematically giving students greater access to relevant information or rehearsing them on weak skills it becomes possible to focus remediation on areas that the student, tutor or software has diagnosed as requiring attention in relation to language learning.

Reflection

By giving the student access to records of their past working, the responses of the peers, tutors and systems they were working with, and by providing them with tools with which to annotate and file such work, it becomes possible to support systematic reflection on what they have learnt and on their own learning processes.

Memory Protheses

By giving students comprehensive access to their past computer mediated work and by providing them with appropriate search engines it becomes possible for students to have the self confidence to be very selective and focused about what they chose to attempt to memorise at any point in time, thus supporting much greater cognitive economy on the part of the learner.

Scaffolding

By tracking student learning gains and by human or system dialogue with the learner it becomes possible to dynamically vary the level of scaffolding provided for learners.

Tackling the hypothetical

By making it possible for students to set up counterfactual situations in simulations or to break laws in symbolic reasoning systems it becomes possible for students to investigate the fundamental principles which underpin formal scientific, mathematical and other models.

Time travel

By facilitating 'time travel' as a matter of routine in simulations and databases it becomes possible to help learners augment their understanding by focusing on the key issues of chronology and causality.

Autonomy

By taking the learner's viewpoint when designing instructional software it becomes possible to give the learner greater control over the degree to which there are external interventions in their learning processes.

Pacing

By providing a 'clock' based on the planned work of a cohort of learners or on an appropriate instructional design it becomes possible for learners to increase their motivation when engage in sequences of learning activity over longer time periods such as terms and years.

Redundancy

By encoding the same learning material using different media elements it becomes possible for heterogeneous groups of learners with different learning styles and media preferences to study the same curriculum content.

Motivation

By addressing issues of intrinsic and extrinsic learner motivation explicitly in the design of learning sequences supported by instructional software, and in the design of educational interfaces, it becomes possible to enhance motivation in ways that depend on the characteristics of the individual learner.

Group working

By supporting synchronous or asynchronous group working modes and by appropriate choice of design to support competitive, collaborative or complementary activity it becomes possible for learners to work in teams and to acquire higher order learning skills from each other.

Knowledge integration

By taking a chronological view when designing instructional software, by deliberately incorporating appropriate elements of media redundancy and by planning for student use of memory prosthetics it becomes much possible for the learner to integrate diverse knowledge acquired at different times.

Access

By incorporating diverse prosthetics in learner interfaces and by designing for learner autonomy and pacing it becomes possible to extend access to learners who cannot take advantage of conventional modes of classroom delivery because of their special social or physical circumstances.

Teacher's role in virtual learning environment

The introduction of a virtual learning environment into any formal educational setting such as a classroom or timetabled course immediately changes the role of the teacher. The students become able to alter radically their pattern of working and learning with respect to both when they work and who they learn with.

Consider the extreme but authentic example of a pupil who used to do geography group project work between ten and eleven on Monday mornings at a particular table with three other designated pupils.

Given access to appropriate conferencing software, the same pupil can work collaboratively with three pupils in other schools in their country on a geography project, and this physically distributed group of learners can used electronic mail and the Internet to get material for their project from peers of their age group who live in the country they are doing their project on.

The timing of the project activity now depends on access to hardware rather the timetabled use of classroom space. If the pupils are in a hardware rich school or have access to networked computers in their homes then the timetabling issue moves to ensuring the right amount of time is devoted over the week or month to the group project. If a school with limited hardware introduces such a project activity then, of course, access to the hardware will have to be timetabled. In either case the role of the teacher will change very considerably with some current aspects of the teacher's role vanishing and new demands on the teacher appearing. The two key classes of activity that will diminish or vanish relate to the teacher no longer acting as the main information and knowledge source and no longer having responsibility for the detail of how pupils spend their time.

Currently, there is an expectation that teachers should be 'oracles', have fairly complete personal mastery of what is being taught, and should be able to guide pupils on how to spend their time hour by hour on a ten minute basis. But the pupil using virtual learning environments has access to a diversity of knowledge sources and ways of easily tracking individual and group learning progress.

Two new teaching roles are required instead. These are the role of learning guide and the role of curriculum designer. They are quite different roles and this change is quite problematic because the role of learning guide or facilitator could be seen as having considerably lower status than a conventional teacher.

The fact that curriculum designers might have the same or higher status than teachers is not going to help very much, because while we can argue that the number of learning guides needed may be similar to the current number of teachers, this will not be true for curriculum design.

The successful curriculum designer who develops a new virtual learning environment will reach audiences of thousands in the same way as a best selling textbook author, and the economics of software design and marketing are such that there will be a natural tendency to aim for a small numbers of educational software products reaching large audiences.

The role of learning guide will be a very demanding one. Students using virtual learning environments pose questions, make comments, develop models, initiate collaborations and engage in a range of other interactions.

The learning guide will have to act as a facilitator for the students, mediating such activity and acting as a mentor and coach for new modes of collaborative learning. Some of the time the learning guide will have to help manage group learning processes and arbitrate as necessary.

Learning guides will themselves naturally use electronic means to share good practice and will contribute to the growing libraries of digital information. These aspects of the learning guide role will not necessarily be confined to professionally trained teachers, and in many cases a peer learner who has already acquired experience and understanding of a particular virtual learning environment will be an appropriate learning guide for the next cohort of learners.

There are other necessary aspects of the role of the learning guide which will require pedagogical expertise.

These include helping groups of learners to adopt realistic expectations, providing appropriate scaffolding for particular learning goals and helping with the timing and pacing of learning activity.

To provide these types of support effectively the learning guide will be a member of the learning community and a peer who will be also be learning and be being seen to learn by the pupils or students. Two aspects of the role of the learning guide will not be integrated into peer learning but will instead remain firmly in the professional domain.

Assessment of students will continue to be required and robust modes of evaluating the contributions of individuals to electronically-mediated group work will have to be devised. Schools and colleges will also have to make choices about investment in hardware, and more particularly software, products and teachers will have to evaluate the offerings of the market with respect to the curriculum goals of their institutions.

The development of usable virtual learning environments usually requires a mix of skills from a range of disciplines including computer science, cognitive psychology, instructional design, artificial intelligence, human computer interaction, educational technology and expertise in the subject being learnt.

Certainly some teachers will join the teams that extend the curriculum through producing new virtual learning environments. The particular roles they are most likely to play in such teams are those of subject matter expert and classroom evaluator.

In the future there might be easy to use authoring tools which require no technical expertise of teachers is a nonsense. Consider what it might mean for there to be authoring tools that made it easy to produce best selling textbooks. Then combine this with the view that marshalling multi-media resources to support a wide variety of learning routes is much more complex than textbook design. This forces the conclusion that non-trivial new virtual learning environments will continue to require the investment of a range of multi-disciplinary skills.

The role of the teacher will be changing as the various forms of integration discussed above proceed. Teachers who adopt the new role of learning guide will have to deal with a new status which is yet to be determined and in some important respects they will become peers with their students and pupils. The ongoing integration of software tools should make it easier for them to adopt this new role in a practical sense.

As teachers change their role they will, from choice or necessity, become much more technologically aware and competent. There will be some continuity of current teaching functions with respect to assessment and resource allocation and, as at present, a small number of teachers will become involved in the creation of new learning materials for the mass market.

Individual robust virtual learning environments are very expensive to produce and they require a communications and hardware infrastructure to deliver. Given the current resource problems facing educational institutions, it becomes critical to analyse how the economics of delivery change as the number of learners being supported grows from tens and hundreds to thousands and millions.

Economically positive aspects of increased scale of use come into play when the learners are able to use the technology to become more autonomous and when it is possible for peer learners to provide mutual coaching and scaffolding support. Attempts to gain economies of scale can easily founder if it turns out that a new piece of software is tied too firmly or obviously to a particular pedagogical subculture, or when a new educational market cannot provide a minimum critical mass of learning guides or coaches.

There is a widespread resistance around the world to educational cultural imperialism and this is certainly rational behaviour when applied to software products marketed to learning communities.

In analysing scaleability it is necessary to have clarity on the range for a reasonable and sensible number of active learners per running instance of a given virtual learning environmentSome types of software are designed for individual use and should support the learner as they manage their learning activity and seek new information resources. A good example would be one of the contemporary generation of browsers for the World Wide Web. Such software is only scaleable if it has integral on-line help and a very high standard of documentation.

While the learners will be able to support each other to an extent, the environment will not succeed without properly designed learner support materials. At the other extreme is software designed to be used at the same time by hundreds, thousand or millions of learners. In this situation the typical learner has a role akin to that of the viewer of a piece of educational television except, of course, that the interaction being observed will very often involve only one or a very small number of the other learners making active contributions at any point in time. At this extreme there may be a formal teaching role that takes advantage of the digital broadcast but there is no reason for these to be especially different from current teaching roles unless they take advantage of an asynchronous learning network or virtual classroom.

The latter approach represents the most mature form of interactive learning environment and typically learners are organised into distinct groups each composed of some twenty to thirty learners. There is a strong consensus amongst workers in this area that virtual classrooms and similar approaches that take advantage of computer mediated conferencing become unmanageable if you allow the group size to get very much larger than the number found in conventional classrooms. This style of approach supporting between ten and a hundred will not scale, as the number of teachers, learning guides or coaches will have to increase linearly with the number of students in the same way that one finds in other forms of education.

But the learning support task is not the conventional teaching role and a cascade or tree cluster model for developing and training new learning guides may be applied. In this case a form of bootstrapping can occur with the virtual learning environment being first used to train their learning guides. So this approach is potentially cheaper but involves the greatest role change for the teacher.

The fourth category involves two to ten learners working together simultaneously but perhaps in different physical locations with a system dynamically programmable multi-user virtual reality. In a situation like this the scaleability question will depend both on the usability and learnability of the virtual learning environment and on cognitive challenge given by the task or goal being addressed by the group of learners.

In many of the virtual learning environments currently being experimented with in this sort of style the learning support demands appear to be much more acute than those found in the conventional classroom. At present arguments for adopting such environments will depend either on the educational quality of the experience offered the learner or on a finesse to the learning support problem that makes use of peer learning or the use of past student work as exemplars or as models for current students. Because of the ease of potential reuse of material in digital form, small groups of students, who are for example accessing global digital libraries together, can work much more effectively if they start from relevant work from past students with similar backgrounds.

The good news for the current generation of teachers is that because of the scaleability issues discussed above, virtual learning environments cannot be assumed to offer a cheap way of replacing or doing without teachers. Educational policy makers will be obliged to convince themselves that these new approaches offer unique educational benefits, and then consider how much support different numbers of learners working together or separately will need.

The average level of support will vary with the type of software being deployed and the number of learners who are active. The bad news for the current generation of teachers is that some forms of learning environment will represent an economically viable way of replacing some of the didactic functions which many teachers enjoy.

Virtual learning environments are a reality. Visualisation and model building help small groups of learners understand together very hard concepts in mathematics and science. There are systems that support classroom-size groups of learners engaging in high quality open-ended discussion and advanced project work.

With respect to the technology, there would be the continuing integration of information and communication technologies, the integration of synchronous and asynchronous modes of use and the integration of tools for searching through and constructing libraries of digital learning materials.

The pedagogical approach is to view learning as a constructive cognitive activity that must be understood in relation to its social and cultural setting. In applying such a constructivist approach to using technology the best way forward is to build and test rather than theorise about innovative virtual learning environments. The role of the teacher will change as the three forms of technology integration take place.

There will be some continuity of current teaching functions with respect to assessment and resource allocation and, as at present, a small number of teachers will become involved in the creation of new learning materials for the mass market. But the great majority of teachers who adopt the new role of learning guide will have to negotiate a new status and in some important respects they will become peer learners of their students and pupils.

There is no simple answer to the economies of scale question. Some approaches scale much more easily than others and it is necessary to analyse each new virtual learning environment with respect to how many students should be associated with each running instance and what the effective human learning guide support arrangements should be.

Creating Learning Networks

Ongoing professional development through the establishment of collaborative learning networks promise to provide incentives for change not perceived before. An important driving force behind these professional networks are the emerging information and communication technologies. Today's world is rapidly moving towards a more open and global society, bringing opportunities for economic growth, peace, human rights and international partnership, but also creating new sets of problems related to changing patterns of labour, multi-cultural societies and environmental disruption. Knowledge is dynamic: what is true today, may have no value tomorrow. At the same time, access to information is perceived to be vital to economic development and power.

The increasing variety of media sources and growing amount of accessible data create a situation in which the individual or community at the receiver end is increasingly becoming responsible for the selection of relevant, useful and accurate information, a responsibility requiring critical media awareness. While information and communication technologies more and more allow for many people to also generate and disseminate information, and thus play an active role in the processes of interaction between professionals, laymen, learners, policy makers, peers, etc., it requires skills and knowledge and access to resources to effectively do so.

Pressures of the contemporary age require people, communities and institutions to continually develop and utilise different kinds of knowledge frameworks, value systems, intelligences and skills in order to make sense of, adapt to and contribute to change in constructive and non-violent ways. There is a need for people to learn how to deal with the changing demands of our society and at the same time, develop the capacity that allows them to change in order to take control. Learning has become an essential condition for personal and societal growth and development.

During the 20th century, education received more and more attention as a major factor contributing to development, mainly driven by the thinking represented in the emerging human capital and modernisation theories. This resulted in expansion of school enrolment and increases in educational expenditure in absolute terms on a global level. Such actions have been stimulated and reinforced by international conferences such as the World Conference on Education for All and the mid-decade meeting of the International Consultative Forum on Education for All. While these actions have to be applauded for the achievements in achieving higher enrolment figures, we see at the same time how schools increasingly fail to provide the learning opportunities required in today's communities. Both human capital theory and modernisation theory have been criticised on their weak argumentation regarding the role of schooling in development.

Schooling is mostly adaptive in nature and reproduces existing social and economic systems rather than triggers change and development. Apart from theoretical critique we can observe now, in the late 90s, that also reality has proven us wrong in our belief in the expansion of the school system as such. In the 70s and 80s, Africa had the highest growth figures in educational enrolment at all levels as well as in expenditures for education as a percentage of GNP. In the 90s these figures have stagnated or even declined. In Africa more than 200 million adults are illiterate (44% of the adult population) and the gross enrolment figures in sub-Saharan Africa are 73,1% for primary level, 23,1% for secondary and 3,3% for tertiary level education. The Africa example teaches us that society's learning needs cannot be addressed only by expanding the formal education system but require new ways to look at both access to and quality of education and learning. Rather then only aiming at the building of more schools and training more teachers to allow for higher enrolment figures, a new perspective is required in which we look at how we can create more open and flexible learning opportunities for all.

It is not so important to have as many people as possible in the classroom, rather we believe that the focus should be on the creation of learning environments, as the Amman Affirmation states:

> 'Given the trend toward more open societies and global economies, we must emphasise the forms of learning and critical thinking that enable individuals to understand changing environments, create new knowledge and shape their own destinies. We must respond to new challenges by promoting learning in all aspects of life, through all institutions of society,

> in effect, creating environments in which living is learning.'

We are living in a world that is dramatically different from our world just six years ago, the time it takes to for an individual to complete primary school. The rate of change is so dramatically that it no longer suffices to teach our children what we think is important. Rather than us preparing our children for their life tomorrow, we have to give this task in the hands of the coming generations themselves. Whereas in the past, change could be managed through generational processes, each generation preparing the conditions for the next generation to adapt to change, this process has now become and intra-generation one. It is essential that each person develops a concept of 'self-as-learner.' Learning to learn involves developing oneself to engage in critical reflection and creative thinking. Such processes can be stimulated through approaches that are learner-centred, self-directed and focus on problem- and activity-based learning. A big challenge lies in stimulating the learners' ability to build and enhance their own knowledge structures that are flexible and adaptable.

People are part of different communities with diverse social and cultural backgrounds and are therefore at times exposed to different situations from which one can learn. Only a part of their time children spend in the classroom; in developing countries and also in urban areas of less developed countries, they are watching 3-4 hours of TV per day. Teachers often feel they are competing with modern media for children's attention and interest. Rather then trying to compete, we believe that the teacher can very much benefit from such 'outside' influences in a constructive way.

In order to create effective learning opportunities, learning process facilitators should build on these experiences and stimulate the development of an integrated model of learning that involves classroom teaching as well as interaction with other learning channels such as family members, others in the community, social experiences, other learners and a variety of media. Within this framework, teachers should be encouraged to link up more actively with the communities they belong to and build a multichannel learning approach. At the same time, teachers should assist learners in developing a critical eye in judging the varying, and sometimes conflicting, information that these different channels provide.

As learning can no longer be viewed as a ritual that one engages in during only the early part of one's life with an occasional refresher course but rather a continuous necessity, opportunities for learning need to be provided that are more flexible and open to the specific needs of individuals or groups of learners. People should have the opportunity to engage in learning whenever and where-ever required without being hindered by barriers such as age, distance, time, social, economic or cultural circumstances.

If we take the existent school establishment and look at what opportunities there are to really do things different, rather then tinker with ongoing practices, or worse, try to do more of the same, teachers are the actors who really are in the position to make things happen, given their central role in the current practice of education. The idea of teachers as change agents is key to many education reform programmes that emphasise the importance of improved teacher training. But somehow such programmes never seem to have the expected results. Teachers constitute the 'largest single group of trained professionals in the world'. A tremendous challenge when we realise that they are also often considered the largest force against change. Teachers often operate in isolation, they mostly have no opportunity to reflect on their own practice or to exchange experiences and ideas with colleagues due to high work pressure and/or the necessity to have more than one full time job.

At the same time, those teachers who are enthusiastic, capable and highly motivated, are frustrated with their contribution to change and having a long-lasting impact, as often a supporting and understanding environment seems to be lacking. Triggering teachers to initiate processes of change involves not the imposition of measures by the school management but rather should be the result of self motivated processes of learning by the teachers. Fullan, Bennet and Rolheiser-Bennet identify four aspects of the teacher as learner which are crucial in the improvement of classroom practice and functioning of schools as a whole. We would like to go further and argue that the following four aspects promote a process of opening up the classroom as learning environment, merging the activities that take place in surrounding communities with what is happening in school:

- development of the instructional repertoire in teachers: the range of instructional strategies and capability to put to work a variety of learning channels;
- development of reflective practice facilitates clarity, meaning and coherence for the teacher in regards to his/her functioning and role in the learning process;

— stimulation of research activities to develop an attitude of investigation and exploration, widening the horizon of the teaching practice beyond the constraints of the classroom;

— promotion of collaboration with colleagues nearby and long distance enables teachers to exchange experiences, receive and give ideas, feedback and assistance.

Rather then trying to mould teachers' attitudes along these lines, we should seek for opportunities to let teachers become learners, to challenge them in a process of professional development in order to develop those skills and practices that are most constructive in the learning communities they are part of. Such processes should not be seen in isolation, but rather as an integrated approach to professional development and educational reform. Teacher development should aim at strategies that stimulate collaboration and partnership between teacher educators, teachers, specialists as well as learners and their parents.

ICTs and Learning Opportunities

Communication and information technologies (ICTs) have become an integral part of society in many countries, not only in industrialised countries but also more and more on the African continent. These technological developments are contributing to expanding opportunities for engaging in teaching and learning at individual, community and society levels. Through their potential to facilitate communication and access to information, ICTs can contribute to collaboration and partnership and are as such key to professional development and educational reform. Using applications like email, computer mediated conferencing, discussion lists, bulletin boards and the World Wide Web, these new technologies have shown to create opportunities for, among others:

— collaboration among teachers and their partners to break through their traditional isolation; partnership across the globe (children, parents, teachers) for international peace and understanding of global issues related to e.g. cultural diversity and environmental health.

— access to nearly unlimited resources on the Internet and to locally stored information (graphical, audio and text) for the manipulation of materials retrieved or locally produced by users in a variety of ways, for presentation purposes, for experimentation purposes, for exploration purposes, herewith enhancing the development of locally relevant learning and teaching materials;

— learner-centred and self-directed learning approaches.

Learning Network Project

'Creating Learning Networks for African Teachers'is a project that is currently being implemented in the framework of UNESCO's Learning Without Frontiers (LWF) initiative. The project aims to benefit from the emerging powers of modern information and communication technologies to stimulate processes of change within the broader objective of rethinking education and learning. The project aimed to enhance teachers capacity to respond to new challenges to teaching and learning by facilitating and stimulating innovative experiences:

— opening up teacher training colleges to the communities by becoming information, communication and learning resources for educational planners and researchers, for teachers and for specific learning communities;

— changing perceptions among educational planners and policy makers, researchers, teacher educators and teachers, to begin seeing themselves as lifelong learners and agents for transformation in multi-faceted environment.

— involving teachers and others as learners in a process in which they are not anymore passive receivers of education, but instead actively contribute to the definition of their learning needs, the planning and execution of their learning and as such participate in the ongoing process of constructing knowledge useful to themselves and their communities.

The project, still in its pilot stage, will connect a number of teacher training colleges to the Internet in order to develop local, national and regional networks to initiate activities that focus on:

— enhancing dialogue between teacher training colleges, educational planners and policy makers, researchers and practising teachers on issues related to learning and teaching;

— accessing and assessing information on latest concepts, developments and experiments in the field of learning, teaching and education to enhance professional development, building local knowledge structures and stimulate processes of change;

— stimulating the development of locally adapted and relevant curricula, appropriate teaching and learning materials - print based- through group work and groupware, using locally relevant images and sounds;

— promoting the development and implementation of learning projects, targeting different learner groups of the communities around them;

Through the development of these activities, providing room for creative initiatives of teacher trainers and other parties, the project aims at opening up the school system and the development of an approach to learning which is more in line with the needs and requirements of today's African society.

Before implementing the project at a large scale, pilot activities will be initiated in a limited number of countries to assess the feasibility of the proposed activities and to further develop the specific modalities and requirements - in terms of hardware, software, connectivity arrangements, networking partners, training, etc. Zimbabwe was selected as a first country for this pilot project and it is currently experimenting with the first phase of the project. The choice of Zimbabwe was based on its advanced connectivity plans and current attempts to improve the overall quality of its educational system. So far, a team of enthusiastic educators comprising a selection of members of teacher training colleges, the teacher education department at the University of Zimbabwe and the audio-visual and curriculum development unit within the Ministry of Education has received basic training in the use of the

Internet and computers which have been installed and connected by specialists from the country. Currently, an electronic discussion group is being set up for thematic discussions on education issues, relevant in the specific Zimbabwean context and a national web site is being prepared that will facilitate access to learning resources for Zimbabwean teachers.

2

Virtual Classroom

Internet education and training is, at the least, about replacing traditional print-based distance learning with an electronic model: students may still buy a textbook, but other materials are delivered via the Web. Even better, students can now communicate with their tutors, other students, and experts elsewhere. They can find comprehensive Web-based information, chaotic as it is, more current than in any traditional library. They can share voice, images, software, and video screens with other students

The quality of learning can be enhanced through simulation of engineering, scientific, business, social, or medical scenarios. Self-assessment tools can be used to tailor learning paths to individual student needs. Systems for the management of learning online are now becoming available. Other systems, for tutor management, student administration, information searching, and automated assessment are being developed or are available in-house.

Online providers are developing Web-based reading lists and forums by discipline. The business of learning, which is so information intensive, is succumbing to information systems. Most of this technology is available now, but the curriculum hasn't caught up - and converting existing courses requires a massive effort beyond most institution's budgets. The broadband services are supporting quality voice and video conferencing, and the cost issue is being address through mass services such as cable TV. Commerce is exploding as businesses discover the virtue of contestability of supply and reduced transactions costs.

The number of degree courses being offered on the Internet is exploding - from a handful a year ago, to thousands today. Although the picture is chaotic and embryonic, a few trends seem clear:

— The transition from local to global education services is occurring and is irreversible

— Private investment in and income are becoming more important - governments are everywhere resiling from their commitments to funding free or even subsidised education

— The demand for education and workplace training is still increasing, and is seen as a driver of economic growth and innovation

— The resulting competition will have some or all of the following effects

— Rationalisation of courses

— The growth of brand as a determinant of student choice

— Contestability of supply of tutoring services

— A rising investment requirement for quality multimedia learning tools

— Specialisation, as institutions seek market differentiation

— Mergers, alliances, and closures

There are other possibilities in the longer term, some of them dramatic in their implications . Of course, a more comprehensive view of the future of higher education is needed if we are to make sensible responses to the impact of globalisation. In the face of cost, brand, quality, technology and demand pressures, universities must develop responses just as businesses always have when threats emerge. For many, the threats have always been there.

The differences now are in the way fundamental truths of a geographical or cultural franchise are being overturned through low cost, interactive communication. The competitor is no longer just the established but arrogant campus across town, or the upstart but student-oriented campus 100 km west: it is the 2000 or more aggressive, lean institutions with a presence on the Web - some of them with brands we can never develop in a lifetime, and perhaps with a greater commitment to customer service than we have had in the past.

We are talking here about nothing less than a re-engineering of a teaching process largely untouched over several centuries; about dramatic changes to the economics of education; about shifts in the power of accreditation; and about private involvement in an industry which hitherto has resisted such intrusions except at the edges. The student will demand, even is demanding more colourful lectures, more interactive tutorials, and a generally more entertaining learning experience than his predecessor.

Governments are tiring of their obligation to fund higher education. What was once an unquestioned commitment has been bundled together with unemployment benefits, pensions, and health as a commitment to special groups only, to be minimised to reduce government involvement in all but the most essential of services.

Some economies have been made in the system, notably by reducing tutorial activity. However, cost reduction in a service business such as education is difficult, and institutions have generally targeted revenue by pursuing high growth/high fee courses in business, law, and information technology.

We have yet to see the impact of the increases in fees on enrolments, but even a small drop in enrolments will be critical for some institutions and disciplines, because it significantly erodes margin in what is essentially a fixed cost business. Many institutions will be unable to afford the redundancy payouts necessary to adjust to the lower demand, even without considering the need to lift salaries to retain skilled staff. Subjects such as law would be expected to be most heavily affected, and this is a high margin subject. At the same time as this is happening, the requirement to offer expensive multimedia courses is increasing.

The consequence of these changes is that universities must seek to lift revenue, because operating costs scale fairly accurately with enrolments, and therefore with grant revenue. Further, the method used to lift revenue must use leverage: it must present opportunities which do not require a proportionate increase in investment. They must also seeks partners with financial resources equal to the new tasks.

Increasingly, the power of employment rests with the markets, and only the elite university brands. The generic brand strength of degrees has been eroded by overuse, by a loss of exclusivity. As in other social measures, a stratification into the lowly and the elite is taking place.

Degrees without exclusivity are declining to the point where they are increasingly discounted in the eyes of would-be employers, and job performance is replacing them as a qualification. The information technology industry has long been a precursor of other industries in this respect. Even the once priceless MBA has been scarred and sullied, with the effect of raising the status of the few and debasing the rest.

Virtual Classroom

The World Wide Web and other Internet-based collaborative tools have significantly enhanced the ability to train and educate electronically. Whether the materials are a stand-alone tutorial or a full-fledged on-line workshop, the Web provides significant new functionality in transmitting information to the student and providing forums for exchange. When integrated with tools such as listservs, Usenet newsgroups, annotation facilities, and video teleconferencing, the Web can greatly increase students' level of involvement in the training experience. Web provides an effective mechanism for integrating many of these tools into a single interface and is an ideal tool for information which is itself rapidly changing. It revolutionize areas of study through increased opportunities for learning and alternative formats for information.

For example, in US, the Cornell Theory Center (CTC) is a nationally funded high performance computing center founded in 1985 and located in Ithaca, New York. Its mission includes providing supercomputing resources and technical support to researchers at academic institutions and national laboratories across the United States. Educating researchers in effective and efficient use of the rapidly changing technology of high performance computing is a core component of its mission. Over 60% of the users of the facilities are located outside of Cornell University.

Hence, use of an on-line information system and electronic tutorials has been central to the education and training activities from the beginning of the center. It is clear that the internet, with its ability to connect people and information around the world, is already having a significant impact on education at all levels. The lofty goal of an interconnected global schoolhouse across remote corners of the world is getting closer.

Virtual classrooms are being created today for educating scientists, engineers and mathematicians, both researchers and faculty, and will provide needed experience and basic knowledge for use with other student populations in the near future.

The CTC provides educational opportunities for researchers, faculty, and students in the effective use of high performance computing for the exploration of scientific problems. Workshops for new and experienced users of the Center's resources are offered on a regular basis. Workshops include lectures on system features, optimization, introductory and advanced topics in scalable parallel computing, and visualization. Lectures are supplemented by guided hands-on laboratory sessions to ensure that participants gain needed experience.

Over the past 9 years, the Theory Center staff has assisted hundreds of researchers in moving legacy serial codes to vectorized and now parallelized implementations.

On-line educational materials, which include lecture notes and lab exercises, are available through the World Wide Web. These materials are used by the Center's staff during workshops and by others on the Internet who wish to provide instruction on these topics. In addition, the materials provide a handy access point for researchers and students to review concepts that were presented in workshops.

Educational materials also include a set of tutorials especially designed for on-line learning. These tutorials are the recommended starting point for researchers and students desiring to become familiar with the use of the Theory Center's systems and scalable parallel computing. In addition to direct education of users of the facilities, a "train-the-trainer" model is used to leverage the support effort. This is accomplished through the academic affiliates activities, known as the Smart Node Programme.

Each of the more than 90 participating universities sends a consultant to the Theory Center for a one week workshop each year. At the workshop, the consultants are updated on the latest technologies. They then return to their own campus to provide support to local researchers often by re-using the training materials in courses that they offer. The on-line documents and training materials provide continuous access to materials for Smart Node consultants to use in training users at their local campuses. Extensive feedback from the Smart Node consultants over the past seven years has provided ample evidence that the materials are heavily re-used as is and frequently modified and incorporated into local materials to meet specialized needs. This was true even when we were in a 'paper' environment.

With the availability of the Web, this re-use has increased dramatically. Because of the rapidly changing technology in high performance computing, researchers who use the facility need to continually update their knowledge of state-of-the-art computational science techniques.

As these users are spread across the United States, it is not feasible for frequent visits to the Theory Center to attend workshops. Educating researchers in concepts and approaches to parallel processing is a staff-intensive effort.

Electronic Education System

While the hardware and software vendors sometimes supply user documentation in electronic format, it is often "command" oriented, but the users often require "task" oriented materials (e.g., the user needs to learn how to run a batch job, without prior knowledge of the names of the five commands involved) and each vendor uses a different interface for access to on-line materials. Even now that computing vendors are creating World Wide Web servers, they are slow to include user documentation, but instead concentrate on marketing information. For all of these reasons the center have made use of an electronic user documentation system since its founding in 1985.

The Theory Center on-line information system contains educational materials in a variety of formats. They have developed more than 140 items specifically designed to be instructional tools that are referenced thousands of times each month. This electronic education system not only serves the CTC researchers, but also the international research audience, and provides materials that other educators can incorporate into their courses. The types of educational materials in the on-line information system.

Tutorials: Electronic tutorials have been available for more than nine years. Tutorials are intended to be short, self-contained instructions on a specific topic (e.g., use of an optimization subroutine library). Each tutorial contains a short description, step-by-step instructions in using the utility, and an example code that can be executed. Researchers can read the tutorial and try the example, possibly taking the example code to use as a template for their own problem. These tutorials are task-oriented, not command-oriented.

Lab exercises: Lab exercises have been provided in electronic format for the past two years. These exercises are intended to supplement lectures given at a workshop. The solutions to lab exercises are provided in a separate file to encourage the student to solve the problem instead of following the cookbook instructions found in a tutorial. Placing the lab exercises on-line has allowed workshop participants to more easily continue to work on the problems after returning home. Also, the on-line versions can be kept up-to-date where hardcopy lab exercises quickly become out-of-date.

Lecture notes: During the fall of 1994 the centre began to maintain a complete set of lecture notes on-line.

Formatted as a traditional "overhead foils", lecture notes are frequently a list of bullets which provide a guideline for the lecturer to use in presenting the materials.

Lecture notes may not contain full details of the topic, but usually contain many references to other electronic materials for more information. In addition to providing continuous access to these materials for workshop attendees and other trainers, the centre has been experimenting with using NCSA Mosaic and Netscape as the mechanism for presenting the lecture.

The students can follow the lecture on a terminal in front of them or can see the instructor's monitor displayed with a large screen projection system. Future improvements to the system can be carried out to incorporate images, animation, and user-interaction forms into the documents. It is hoped that to use the more advanced functionality provided by the Web and emerging search technologies to better integrate training materials, hardware and software documentation, on algorithm design and related research projects. Changes in these areas will continue the evolution to an increasingly effective on-line information system.

Plans for the Virtual Classroom

Distance education, in the form of a course offered across the Internet, is a logical next step for the Theory Center. The course is distinct from user-initiated, independent accesses to the on-line materials because it will have an instructor and a registered group of participants. This brings together a community of learners into a virtual classroom where they can interact with each other. The goal is to create a virtual classroom, using methods that will fully engage the students in the learning process through an interactive, dynamic environment involving the student, on-line materials and an instructor.

Education through the net

There are many topics that need to be explored before being able to offer complete workshops over the Internet. These range from technical considerations to sociological aspects of learning without the existence of a physical classroom. Much study has already been done in distance education. While distance education can provide efficient utilization of scarce resources, more fair distribution of knowledge, and timely dissemination of new knowledge, limitations in its effective use exist.

On-line instructors may need to take more time for the electronic course. Limits to the number of students may be required to maintain quality interaction. While generalizations in the effectiveness of distance education are dangerous, a common set of advantages and disadvantages are emerging. The Web solves some problems of traditional distance education and brings new issues to the forefront. A leading effort in exploring this emerging world is the Global Network Academy.

The Theory Center is facing a number of similar issues, but will also have some unique situations related to the field of instruction and the network-sophistication of the intended audience. Some of the issues addressed for the pilot course follow.

Target audience: With traditional workshops, attendance is limited by the physical size of the training facility (about 50 students). Normally this means that attendees are users and potential users of the facilities—

researchers whose backgrounds, computing experiences, and expectations are somewhat similar. With an electronic course, the size of the class will be limited by other non-physical factors such as staffing requirements for account administration, limited consulting support, and CPU resources required for the class laboratory exercises.

Prerequisites: As the centre do for participation in the traditional workshops, they require a basic knowledge of UNIX. With workshops held in the training facility they know what type of computer hardware, software and network connection the students will have. For an electronic course an Internet connection is required. This requirement could exclude some students from participation, but would greatly increase the functionality that the centre can make use of for the materials. Even with a graphical browser, some students may find limited network bandwidth does not provide a satisfactory learning environment.

Learning environment: Extensive feedback from attendees at the traditional workshops indicates there are two benefits to learning in a classroom setting which are independent of the material covered in the course.

— students find that the ability to get away from their other responsibilities and concentrate on learning the course materials greatly increases the amount that they learn and retain.

— the interaction with other students and Theory Center staff, whether it is side discussions during the lab periods or simply listening to questions asked by others, often results in people rethinking their own computing techniques and suggest new solutions to their problems.

An electronic course needs some of the same attributes in order to ensure that students find the experience worthwhile so that they complete the course. There needs to be some sense of an "instructor" for the students to interact with and the ability for the entire class to participate in questions and answers.

Audio-Visual Equipments

In a physical classroom there is a standard set of audio-visual equipment and tools available to the instructor. These might include a chalkboard, overhead projector, video cassette player, possibly a sound system, and even the textbook. Professional instructors know how to make best use of these tools.

The virtual classroom needs equivalent equipment and tools in the form of network-based software applications. Some of these virtual tools have a relatively long history on the Internet and provide obvious applications. Other are still emerging and their potential use in a virtual classroom is not yet understood. With the appropriate design, the student should be able to take advantage of these tools without leaving the comfort of their favorite Web browser interface. Some of those considered for the classroom are;

The textbook: Many courses have a textbook used to guide the direction of the course or for background material. While the on-line materials provide some of this function, these may sometimes not provide all of the details that a users needs. In the area of high performance computing an example of a useful electronic textbook is the Computational Science Education Project sponsored by the U.S. Department of Energy. The growth of electronic publishing on the Internet should ensure a good supply of electronic textbooks over the coming years.

The chalkboard: Even when the lecture materials are prepared in advance and made available to the student, most instructors make use of a chalkboard for further clarification of a point. In an electronic course, the instructor might make use of the shared whiteboard offered by a tool like NCSA Collage to answer a question from a student. Such tools allow images to be displayed, manipulated, annotated, and shared between two people or among a whole group.

Video cassette recorder: Use of mpeg movies and audio clips can be effective additions to textual materials. For the course on scalable parallel computing the center might create a "cartoon" to illustrate how messages are passed between processors in a distributed system or record the animated output of a parallel trace tool. Audio clips of the instructor might be helpful in some instances to describe a particularly difficult point. Either can add some needed relief for what might otherwise be rather dry material—just as an instructor in a traditional classroom might use video tape to keep the students' attention.

The sound system: An important part of any physical class setting is the personal interaction as questions are asked by the students. Allowing all students to "hear" the questions and answers helps everyone learn and encourages additional questions to clarify a point. Use of a listserv to redistribute e-mail questions or a usenet newsgroup are simple methods for sharing this interaction. A more dynamic question and answer period could be created using a chat session. For some types of courses a multi-user, text-based virtual reality, also known as a MUD (Multi-User Domain) or MOO (Multi-user domain Object Oriented), might be effective.

Video teleconferencing: If you were watching a chemist describe the intricacies of a folded protein molecule and its interaction with a drug, chances are much information would be transferred through the hand motions and vocal inflections of the chemist. Body language is one component of physical contact that is difficult to convert to pre-packaged text and still images.

Incorporation of these might be accomplished in the future through video teleconferencing technologies over the Internet. The ability to use video teleconferencing could enhance electronic courses not only by transferring these more subtle forms of communication, but also by providing additional visual and audio cues which help the instructor and students to form an informal rapport.

The pencil: One of the most basic visualization tools used in a classroom is the simple pencil. The student uses the pencil to take notes on what is spoken. The instructor uses the pencil to jot down suggestions for future presentations. In the early experiences with providing only electronic copies of the "overhead foils" during a lecture, many students have been frustrated by the inability to take effective notes. Even the annotation capability with the NCSA Mosaic browser is limited by the limitation of annotation only at the full page level, and by the user interface to annotations.

The creation and use of audio-visual tools is still problematic. The same functionality or at least interoperability must be available across all popular graphical user interfaces. Bandwidth limitations to the students desk also makes many of these tool unusable. It is not acceptable to have to limit participation in the virtual classroom to only those with the best Internet access and interface. Just as HTML has provided a standard which allows participation by users with diverse implementations of both low-end and high-end browsers, audio-visual tools require similar standardization.

The Theory Center's first electronic course, Scalable Parallel Computing on the IBM SP2, was designed to introduce students to basic concepts in scalable parallel computing and all five modules use Theory Center lecture notes as the starting point. Additional text has been written to fill in the lecture and there are links to appropriate tutorials and labs (which already exist). Links are added to point to in-depth material on the topic and draw heavily on existing materials such as the Computational Science Education Project and IBM WWW sites. There are homework assignments, electronic tutoring, and an open forum discussion for all students and teachers.

Prerequisites: A familiarity with UNIX, C or FORTRAN, graphics capable device and sufficient network bandwidth to download images

Module 1—Getting started: the Cornell Theory Center Computing Environment: The student are introduced to the CTC computing environment by familiarizing them with the extensive on-line information system. Specifically, policies, hardware configuration, and training materials are highlighted.

Module 2 - Introduction to Scalable Parallel Computing: This module introduces the student to basic concepts in parallel processing. Performance expectations and limits to scalability are discussed. Students are executed and time existing serial and parallel code to reinforces these concepts.

Module 3 - Message Passing Basics: This module presents concepts in message passing such as latency, bandwidth, computation to communication ratio, barriers and collective communications. It provides an overview of message passing libraries on the SP2, including MPL, MPI, Linda and Express.

Module 4 - PVM: Since these students also do some of their computing on other platforms, it is critical to instruct in the basics of a portable message passing library. PVM is the most widely used and the basic commands and sample programs are explored. The student parallelizes an existing program using PVM. Resulting speedups are shared across the class.

Module 5 - Advance PVM on the SP2: Additional libraries are discussed and more advanced codes introduced. Students required to run two sample codes and create their own parallel program, demonstrating significant speedup through parallelism.

The Theory Center continues to investigate use of on-line information systems for providing effective distance learning opportunities for students and scientists in the areas of computational science and high performance computing.

Learning through the WWW

The World Wide Web is a popular and useful instructional medium for a number of reasons. It is easily accessible, it supports flexible storage and display options, it provides a simple yet powerful publishing format and a means to incorporate multiple media elements. Interestingly, instructional effectiveness is not a proven characteristic for World Wide Web courseware and in many instances delivery via the WWW can impede rather than enhance learning when compared to conventional publishing forms.

The hypermedia format used by the WWW has received wide acclaim and its potential as a learning tool is derived from the nature of the learning that it supports. It facilitates student-centred approaches creating a motivating and active learning environment. It supports and encourages browsing and exploration, learner behaviours that are frequently associated with higher-order learning. The nature of information organisation in hypermedia appears to closely mimic human memory, and retrieval methods closely resemble human thought processes.

Hypermedia facilitates a very natural and efficient form for information retrieval. These and other advantages offered by the medium have created considerable enthusiasm among learning theorists and teachers, towards the WWW and hypermedia as a learning tool. But as with all instructional technologies, potential and reality are frequently not synonymous.

Hypermedia materials themselves do not teach but provide a medium that with appropriate use can support learning. Learning is achieved through a process of constructing knowledge. When a learner is confronted with new knowledge, the learner's intentions, previous experiences, and metacognitive strategies are all essential elements in determining what becomes of the knowledge.

The effectiveness in any learning environment is based upon the types and levels of cognitive and metacognitive activity engendered in the learners. It is now widely accepted that learning is enhanced by active environments in which students have cause to be engaged in processing personally relevant content and to be reflective during the learning process.

WWW as an Instructional Tool

Learning is a process that is influenced by, and results from, the interaction of three areas of influence: agent, activity, and world. For example, Brofenbrenner provides similar descriptions for these influences such as person, process and context approach.

In terms of the instructional design for interactive multimedia programs, a there is the need of a framework with three mutually constitutive elements: the learner, the implementation and the interactive multimedia program to be useful in describing the roles and responsibilities within the learning process.

The three elements correspond to the role of the teacher, learner and the materials themselves, in the instructional setting. When this framework is applied to the design of WWW multimedia materials, key factors and strategies for each of the elements can be identified. While the factors for learner and implementation are quite consistent with other interactive media, within the WWW materials there are a number of important and unique attributes that can be considered.

Designing WWW Documents

Print based instructional materials have served well in the past in support of student-centred independent learning. In recent times, the move to computer-based learning environments has been taken to improve the perceived interactivity of the materials.

There are unique advantages among print and computer-based materials and the WWW appears to provide a means to make the most of the opportunities afforded by each. Some critical considerations in designing electronic instructional and informational materials include organisation, orientation, navigation, presentation and interactivity.

Organisation

A problem facing the WWW designer is choice of the strategy that should be employed to organise the material. While hypermedia describes a particular type of learning environment, there are several forms of exposition that assume this title. The different forms of hypermedia can be described through a continuum describing the nature of the linking involved.

At one end of the continuum, the links are minimal and simply act to connect nodes in a specified sequence. This form of hypermedia closely resembles conventional text and is referred to as linear. In its use, the learner is encouraged and in most cases compelled to follow an instructional sequence planned by the instructor. In hypermedia environments, there is potential to create materials with varying degrees of linearity.

Further along the continuum, the links tend to form a hierarchical structure, giving learners more freedom in the choice of path through the materials. At the extreme, hypermedia can provide a totally unstructured learning environment with multiple links between associated nodes. In this environment, learners are free to move between associated nodes through referential links and very little structure is imposed and in evidence. The choice of information organisation for WWW materials depends on the nature of the intended learning outcomes.

A useful guide for selecting the form of hypermedia most suited to the nature of intended learning outcomes by suggesting instructional strategies against knowledge acquisition aims. When the instructional forms of the different forms of hypermedia are matched against the continuum describing instructional strategies, it is evident that when the materials seek to develop students' initial knowledge, for example, facts, procedures and rules of discourse, linear linking is an appropriate hypermedia form. For this type of learning, it is appropriate to create materials with a strong structure that present information in a planned and considered fashion.

In using these materials, learners are required to follow an instructional sequence set by the teacher. For higher levels of knowledge, for example, developing an understanding of concepts and principles, the less structured hierarchical and referential linking are more appropriate.

In such instances, students are guided by such factors as their prior knowledge and readiness to assimilate new material. When building on an existing knowledge base, learners can benefit from the freedom to browse and explore, to inquire and seek responses to their own questions rather than following a pre-determined path of instruction.

Orientation

One of the major problems with the use of hypermedia as an instructional form when compared to print materials, is the orientation of the learner within the learning environment. Orientation describes the means by which users are able to identify their current position in the system, how they achieved that position and how to return to a previous position. Disorientation is a problem which is frequently observed in studies of hypermedia users and a problem which significantly limits instructional outcomes.

Electronic learning materials can easily conceal much of the information they contain and it is important in the design process to provide the learner with a means to orient and move freely within the information space. A number of strategies are available to the WWW developer to aid orientation within learning materials. These include:

> Placement cues In linear sequences, the use of bars or graphs are commonly used to indicate the distance and placement of the learner in the instructional sequence. These bars are created as graphical elements and are interspersed within the text to provide visual cues.

Hierarchies and Indices: These structures provide access to the information nodes within a system together with an overall structure for the learner that is reinforced as nodes are selected and viewed. The use of frames and targetable windows provide a means for materials to continually display these structures as content is selected and accessed. A number of tutorial guides on the WWW provide good exanmples of this feature.

Semantic Nets Learning can be enhanced when connections and associations between related information are recognised and made specific. The use of image maps as tools by which information nodes can be accessed and selected provide a linking structure and reinforce associations and connections between the contained information as well supporting learner orientation. The CNN Newsroom uses a concept map as alternative means to seek links.

Navigation

It is important when designing for the WWW to employ standard and intuitive ways to move between nodes. Conventional instructional materials require few operational skills on the part of the learner while WWW materials employ many functions and features that can distract learner from the task at hand. It is important in designing materials to minimise the negative impact of poor interface design.

When learners are compelled to think and consider how an interface operates when undertaking a learning task, their attention is split and the mental effort required to attend to information from multiple sources lessens that which can be applied to the actual learning task. At the same time, if learners are not comfortable with the system, its instructional advantages can be lost.

There are a number of guidelines suggested by authors which can act to minimise the amount of mental and cognitive activity associated with controlling the interface. A need for simplicity and consistency in design. When screens change, the only things that change should be the information to which the learner is being directed.

Buttons and controlling features should remain in the same place and should be intuitive rather than clever in their design.

Typographic clues, colour changes and unnecessary graphics all have the potential to distract and should be used sparingly. In terms of text display, distinct guidelines exist to guide hypermedia development.

Critical aspects in WWW content presentation are the text structure and its readability. Coherence in text is assisted by the use of a well-defined structure and appropriate cues. Readers find coherent and well-structured text easier to read than that which is ill-structured.

Structured text provides information in a sequential fashion with elements such as overviews, and a consistent format to which subsequent text can be added. The following paragraphs describe some useful strategies that can be used in developing hypermedia that lead to well structured, coherent and readable texts.

Text structure: Text structure can be aided by the use of cues and overviews. The use of indices and tables showing the structure and relationship between nodes is a useful strategy for this. Many systems use nets to demonstrate the structure and organisation of information and to aid learners in gaining a sense of global structure.

Readability: The readability of a document is a measure of the ease with which a reader is able to comprehend what is being read. There are a number of ways to increase readability of the printed text At the surface level, difficult terms can be linked to nodes that provide further explanation and description, for example, clicking on a word to find its meaning. As an aid to increasing understanding of deeper meaning structures, literal and inferential questions can be placed with paragraph summaries to help the learners to reflect and consider what has been read. While these forms of cues can also be provided in some ways with conventional materials, they can form a natural part of a hypermedia system readily available to those students who seek to employ them while providing no distraction to those who do not need them.

Fragmentation: A number of studies have revealed that fragmentation of information and learning material occurs when it is presented as discrete elements. Fragmentation results in a lack of associative and interpretative contexts and can create a document that appears to the user as a series of discrete rather than coherent information elements. There are several ways to overcome the possibility of learners perceiving fragmentation in a hypermedia system. Most links in hypermedia serve two purposes: to show a relationship exists between two nodes and to provide a path between them.

There should be some distinction made in these two tasks. When links show the form of association they represent as well as providing the means to traverse, navigation is enhanced as an associative context for linked nodes. New nodes can be shown in concert with their predecessors thus establishing a coherence and semantic relationship enabling a common mental representation by the learner. Paraphrases and summaries also enhance learning by helping to reduce the fragmentation caused by the division of the content into hypertext nodes.

Interactivity

The term, interactivity, describes the forms of communication that a medium supports enabling dialogue between the learner and the instructor and is an important attribute of technology-supported educational environments.

With computer-based learning environments, communication between instructor and students are constrained by the technology. The intelligence of the technology is used in place of the instructor and exchanges are made between the learner and the programmed instructional system.

The interactions in electronic learning environments are able to enhance learning through the feedback they provide and the context and purpose they are able to encourage support. Most writers agree that clicking on paths and navigating through a WWW instructional sequence is not representative of interactivity. Until recently, interactivity has been difficult to achieve with WWW documents with most attempts making creative use of limited opportunities.

Some strategies that have been used successfully to create the essence of interactivity in WWW learning materials include the provision of model answers and e-mail communications. More recently, other forms of interactivity have come to be supported by WWW documents.

The use of Common Gateway Interface (CGI) scripts at the server enables designers to create forms within documents by which learners can enter responses and receive programmed feedback. This feature has been used widely in the creation of multiple choice and short answer tests which can be automatically marked and has the capacity to support record-keeping for more advanced student diagnostics.

New developments in client-side processing applications have led to enhanced interactive capabilities for the WWW. The advantage of client-side processing is that learners can receive immediate feedback to interactions. There are many ways in which the role of the learner can be varied within an instructional setting to influence and enhance learning outcomes.

Collaboration

A majority of contemporary computer-based learning reflect the belief that the interactions will, and should be, made by a single user. However research studies have shown that there are clear educational advantages to be derived from collaborative activities among students.

The implications of this for WWW materials are that interactions and activities that engage higher-order thinking and critical reflection need to be included and opportunities presented to enable group and team work. The communications component of the WWW provides unique opportunities to enable forms of communicative and collaborative activities among networked learners.

Computer-based learning programs frequently subdivide skills into small sections which are then taught systematically in a logical order. This often results in the processes requiring little thought as the students can deduce the answers correctly from the preceding section without a real understanding of the subject. Students know information must be relevant because it is in the same section. There is no need for reflection. More effective environments require students to reflect upon a much broader base of knowledge to solve their problem.

The simple fact of being adjacent to a particular topic would be no guarantee that the information is relevant to the problem. In order to solve the problem or complete the task, the student would be required to reflect upon the whole resource by predicting, hypothesising, and experimenting to produce a solution. The increased use of hierarchical and referential links and associations in documents reduces the linearity of the instructional pathway. Activities that encourage reflection and metacognition through increased levels of learner control can assist students to focus more attention onto their own thought processes.

Most computer-based learning programs are designed to be used quietly with the learner selecting, pointing and clicking in silence. Being able to speak the vocabulary and tell the stories of a culture of practice is fundamental to learning and yet the use of many WWW documents allows the knowledge to remain tacit. More effective learning environments ensure that the resources are used within a social context with students working in groups, discussing the issues, back, presenting findings, interviewing and debating the issues to ensure that students have the opportunity to articulate, negotiate and defend their knowledge. The use of e-mail and other communicative activities supported by the WWW provide opportunities for articulation enabling tacit knowledge to be made explicit.

Coaching describes the action of the teacher in providing guidance and help in a learning setting while scaffolding represents the support provided in the form of skills, strategies and links that the students are unable to provide to complete the task. Enhanced achievement is obtained when the strong support is provided initially and then gradually removed as the student becomes able to stand alone.

Many designers of WWW instructional materials attempt to create documents that are self-contained resources that include everything the student needs to learn a particular topic. However, there are many individual learner characteristics that cannot be accommodated in a single WWW document. There have been some attempts to create intelligent systems for the WWW, for example, adaptive hypermedia, but currently this role is still best performed by the teacher.

The teacher's role in coaching, observing students, offering hints and reminders, providing feedback, scaffolding and fading, modeling, and so on, are powerful enhancements to any learning situation. The implication for the instructional design of WWW materials is that the teacher's coaching role needs to be acknowledged and addressed, with suggestions and strategies planned and taken for implementation with students. Much of this planning is independent of the actual development of the WWW materials

Measures and assessments of achievement and outcomes from instructional settings play an important part in the teaching and learning process. Frequently with computer-based learning, assessment measures bear little semblance to the environment in which the learning has taken place. Assessment can no longer be viewed as an add-on to an instructional design or simply as separate stages in a linear process of pre-test, instruction, posttest; rather assessment must become an integrated, ongoing, and seamless part of the learning environment'. The implications of this for instructional design are that some thought should be given to designing assessment which is concerned with the process as well as the product of involvement with the learning program.

The enhanced interactive capabilities of the WWW provides the means for assessment of student learning to extend beyond conventional essays and examinations. More reliable assessments can take the form of evaluation measures such as portfolios, summary statistics of learners' paths through instructional materials, diagnosis, and reflection and self-assessment. Much of this can be achieved and supported through appropriate design of WWW documents and learning materials.

There are many factors which influence the learning that can be achieved from the use of computer-based learning materials such as CD-ROM based multimedia and materials designed for the WWW. Currently most attention in the design of WWW learning materials, and multimedia, seems to be in the planning and development of the materials themselves. While this is an important activity, it must be accompanied by consideration of two other factors in the learning process, the learners themselves and how the materials will be implemented.

Virtual Advising

With a growing nontraditional, working student population, more students utilizing distance education options, and limited student services resources, advisers are looking at ways to use technology to assist with the process of academic advising.

An investigation of current online support services shows that colleges and universities vary in their development of web based services. As distance education became a prominent feature on the landscape of higher education, a comprehensive network of student support services was destined to follow. Advisors are to "nurture, encourage, inform, and support" students during their academic careers. An academic advising program ideally promotes learning and also encourages students to develop intellectually, physically, and personally. In other words, advisement is not simply the process of selecting classes each academic term, but in fact, when done well, involves many people and departments on campus working as a team.

Current best practices in advisement and technology primarily utilize the World Wide Web. According to the US National Association of Academic Advisor (NACADA) guidelines for developing an advisor's web page, the basis for a comprehensive advising site should include the following elements:

— A clear and concise explanation of core curriculum requirements.

— Advisement usually involves a comprehensive explanation of curriculum requirements and a review of what a student has left to complete.

— Making this information available online will free up some time, will give students greater control and responsibility for the advisement process, and is essential information for students trying to determine course selection if they are unable to meet with an advisor.

— A Frequently Asked Questions (FAQ) section.

Every advisor spends a portion of the day repeating answers to the same questions. Putting answers to FAQs online saves time for staff and gives students access to answers as needed. Informational pages for special populations/self help assistance.

While there are certain common needs among students, there are segments of the population with additional unique concerns. Freshmen, students without declared majors, students on academic probation, and commuters are examples of groups with additional needs for support. Examples of information to include for advisement: career/major information, study skills building worksheets, an explanation of the academic standing policy, information on how to get computer access and technical support.

To generate a more personal environment and provide opportunities for interaction, advisors are experimenting with various forms of electronic communications. If advising were simply a matter of giving students a standardized package of information, there would be no reason to have advisors.

Access to a qualified advisor can be achieved through the use of chat rooms, list serves, and email, to mention a few of the most common methods. Assuming own institution is typical of a mid-sized, regional university, many student services including advisement continue to be campus-bound, face-to-face enterprises. As it has grown, the responsibility for advisement has been divided among various departments on campus.

The web provide the capability to access information at the touch of a button. These advances enhance the advisement process, but we must remain mindful that while the "high tech" of computers should not replace the "high touch" of the advisor, technology can further enhance the advisement process and make services more accessible for the students.

Development of virtual classrooms and universities encapsulates the complexity associated with transforming the solid to the ethereal. The commodification of virtuality for tertiary education relies upon similar meanings becoming associated with this space as are ascribed to the real space of existent campuses. What differs between these spaces is the manner in which communication exchange is undertaken and the compression of time and space that occurs in the virtual environment. The traditional institutional university structure however has not altered its organisational practices in response to this compression.

The monolithic institution continues to utilise traditional Weberian notions of the organisation to contain the unexpected. Efficient workers, business and organisations are configured to possess a economic worth. The organisation orientated towards virtual space however operates in a compressed space in which vast distance and individual elements of real-life are immediately accessible. The associations of time and space formulated according to the scale of weeks, days, hours, minutes seconds is inappropriate for the virtual organisation requiring instead different configurations of scale and differing relationships to time and space.

A reassessment of the economic value measures by these scales is also required. It is for these reasons, that the virtual classroom currently operates as an adjunct to conventional distance learning practices and does not reflect or embrace the full potentials available to the virtual organisation. Today, universities and the manner in which students receive their tertiary education is changing.

Sharing information within an educational context, irrespective of the form it takes, fulfils the specific task of fostering a learning environment and a community of scholars. These issues of pedagogy and the consequent learning outcomes are governed by the rituals of discourse. This discourse restricts and structures the fluidity in which specified learning objectives can be achieved. These structures and restrictions impact upon the form and context of educational activity by which information is transmitted and received within the classroom. This form of information sharing is however quite different to those information systems operating at an administrative level. The distinctions that exist for educational practice are more apparent in real-life universities than those which are currently found within the processes of virtual university. These typers of distinction also hallmarks the difference of real-life from a virtual existence. Specific outcomes, beyond the generation of tertiary graduates, must also be accommodated by such universities. Educational imperatives such as excellence in teaching and international research position must continue to be achieved if the guiding rationale of an academic cultural foundation is to continue. The contemporary practices of universities have dramatically shifted from popular and traditional perceptions of the university.

3

Learning Without Boundaries

Learning is in the process of acquiring entirely new meanings. It serves new purposes, comprising the needs of the young as much as the old in a lifelong and life wide perspective. Learning is an attribute not just of individuals, but of different organismic entities in society at levels ranging from local to global. More than ever has it become a key determinant for the survival of the world, rather than merely a condition for survival and well-being of the individual in the world.

An ever growing variety of technologies offers powerful opportunities to support and develop it. However, the perspective on learning as it transpires from current practice and discourse reflects little of the multiple ways learning can be looked upon in the context of what is known about such issues as lifespan development; complex adaptive systems, cognitive science, mind/brain research; or multiple intelligences. Considerations that people have different learning styles and notions about how learning connects to local culture and knowledge systems are equally often absent from such discourse and practice.

Looking at what the world has achieved in terms of education, one sees an impressive institutional infrastructure linked to a firmly established network of interests. Berenfeld refers in this regard to the monopoly of education. Teachers constitute the "largest single group of trained professionals in the world" Within the existing structure, they are not only a major facilitating factor, whose importance, incidentally, is less and less reflected in the social and material recognition they receive, they are also a leading force against change. "Education is increasingly necessary and less and less possible, due to its cost." This consideration can be found in a piece of advice given to UNESCO's Executive Board at the end of 1993 with the recommendation for UNESCO and the international community to work towards a "world system of open education: Learning Without Frontiers". Such a system should enable "all people throughout the world to obtain access to all forms and levels of education within the context of lifelong education which would establish a continuum between universal primary education and higher forms of education."

Referring to education as a major bulwark of conservatism has become a mere cliché. No wonder that any alternative to the mainstream modality of educational provision, the teacher-classroom-textbook modality, had to fight a hard battle to achieve even a minimum of recognition. Against this background, it is to the credit of distance education that it has been increasingly successful in positioning itself as a valid alternative. To establish its validity, however, distance education had to model itself on the same ideological underpinnings that also condition mainstream educational provision and show that it was equally or more effective or at least nearly as good.

Thus it should be no big surprise that the probably best known definition of distance education as "an educational process in which a significant proportion of the teaching is conducted by someone removed in space and time from the learner" is based on the same assumption that underlies the mainstream educational process, i.e. that a main condition for learning is that there is someone who teaches. Moore and Kearsley advance the following more elaborate definition of distance education:

"Distance education is planned learning that normally occurs in a different place from teaching and as a result requires special techniques of course design, special instructional techniques, special methods of communication by electronic and other technology, as well as special organizational and administrative arrangements."

While this definition clearly puts the emphasis on learning and while it does not explicitly refer to a person who teaches, it is no less based on the notion that teaching is a necessary condition for learning to take place. For this very reason, the two authors express a clear preference for the term 'distance education' over that of 'distance learning'. Such a position is unnecessarily restrictive as it is based on the notion that the best distance education can do, is to approximate as closely as possible the learning-through-delivery-of-teaching model inherent in the face-to-face mode.

Centuries of educational development have not succeeded to avoid that close to a billion people in the world are illiterate, that more than 130 million school-age children do not go to school and that many of those who do, often end up with learning achievements that fail to sustain or that are irrelevant to their needs. There is thus a clear indication that yesterday's educational solutions are inadequate for today's problems and there can hardly be a stronger signal that doing more of the same is not a valid solution. It is equally apparent that today's solutions are an inadequate option in response to the challenges of the future.

The main conception underlying education continues to be that learning is something one does once in a lifetime and that it is essentially undertaken in preparation for the rest of one's life. It is thus best done during the early stages of one's life. For those who, for whatever reason, missed the boat, there are second chance opportunities, often via the distance education mode. Whatever is done in addition to this boils down to learning every now and then in the course of one's life in response to specific needs to maintain or upgrade professional skills or to adapt to new demands of the work environment.

There is no strong notion of lifelong and lifewide learning as an essential ingredient of life itself, as something which is more than, for example, a simple means to acquire a particular skill or to become familiar with a specific area of knowledge. Mainstream educational thinking is still far removed from the "vision of the coming century" expressed in the report of the 'Delors Commission', i.e. "of one in which the pursuit of learning is valued by individuals and by authorities all over the world not only as a means to an end, but also as an end in itself".

To respond to the dual challenge to on the one hand overcome the failures of the past and on the other to be responsive to the demands of the future, the world needs to move beyond fixed modality delivery options based on the teaching-learning dichotomy. It needs to put learning and the learners at the center of its concerns. It needs to break through the barrier of looking at learning as the consequence of something that is being done to people instead of something that is done by and with people. The relationship between learning and empowerment is a dialectic one.

Learning leads to empowerment, but it will do so only if the learning process itself is premised on the notion of the empowered learner. The learning-through-delivery-of-teaching model, whether face-to-face or at a distance, is contrary to that notion. Until a couple of decades ago, learning in preparation for the rest of one's life was still generally a valid option. School systems provided the main mechanisms to put that option into practice. A ministry of education could claim it had things under control if an adequate school system existed and people pertaining to the various socio-economic strata of the population felt they had access to that school system according to their aspirations and needs. People could be reasonably sure that, after completing their education, they were well prepared for the rest of their life. The time to learn was over, and real life could begin. This, however, is no longer the case. In today's world, and that of tomorrow, the notion of learning to earn a living, and even that of learning for life, is no longer a valid one. Learning is no longer for life, but learning is life and life is learning. Learning is pervasive.

Individuals and societal entities - organizations, local communities, cities, whole nations even - are in constant need to adapt to change. While they do so, they generate change themselves. Learning is not only an essential requirement to allow people and groups of people to adapt to change, it is at the same time the most effective mechanism to ensure that change is being generated in a way that takes into account the ecological dimensions of its impact on others. Change occurs at a pace which has brought an essential dimension of unpredictability in the lives of people. It has become impossible to foresee one's life and thus to plan one's education accordingly, as if it were part of a linear sequence of events. Adaptation to change can no longer be managed as a generational process - it has become intra-generational. Most of the existing educational establishment is out of tune with this reality.

The notion of learning as an essential condition of growth of complex adaptive systems is currently perhaps best exemplified by the learning organizations. Survival, gaining and retaining competitiveness, are obviously much more immediately felt urgencies in the business environment than in the traditional closed school environment and its supporting institutions. It is there that one sees complex adaptive systems in action at a scale that may generate interesting models for the reconceptualization of learning environments in general and the diffusion of organizational learning beyond profit making institutions.

This should lead us to think of learning communities - rather than just learning individuals - as crucial elements in the conception of facilitating environments for learning. Most schools, and for that matter also the traditional distance education institutions, are not learning communities. They are simply closed organized structures designed to turn uneducated individuals into educated ones. They do themselves, as social entities, not learn and are not designed to do so. Quite to the contrary, if one considers their tremendous capacity to often totally ignore and resist change, the conclusion would seem to be justified that they have been designed not to learn.

Open Learning Communities

Learning communities in the sense referred to above are essentially open systems. They interact and are in dynamic equilibrium with their environment, i.e. with other learning communities. They are not fixed. Individuals may be part of different learning communities depending on context and circumstance. The term 'distance education' is now often associated with that of 'open learning'. 'Open and distance learning' is thus frequently used as a single concept, suggesting that distance learning is by necessity an open process and that open learning is mainly accomplished in the distance education mode.

The use of terms such as 'open university' and 'open school' adds to the confusion. The dimension of openness of such institutions is often limited. In addition, both 'open learning' and 'distance education' are frequently presented in contrast to and as separate from so-called conventional or traditional education. Distance education has as such little to do with the notion of openness as it appears in the concept 'open learning community'. Systems that use it as a modality can be equally traditional as and no more open than many conventional systems, based on the face-to-face mode. Yet, distance education has much to contribute. Thanks to the development of distance education we now have important experience of self-directed and self-motivated learning and increasingly also of multi-channel approaches, which often include distance learning modalities.

By nature, pen learning communities cannot be established by an outside agent. They are constructed by those who pertain to them. They are themselves the result of a constructivist learning process, involving a variety of partners whose roles can best no longer be dichotomized as either those of learner or teacher. The process of their construction is helped along by the existence of a facilitating open learning environment which contains the essential ingredients and building blocks that learning communities will want to make use of. It is such environments that we must build. In building up propitious environments that are conducive to the generation of open learning one faces a dilemma.

There is important existing infrastructure and practice that one would like to build on. However, part of that same infrastructure and practice reflects much of what is in urgent need to be changed whereas another important part of it has hardly received recognition as belonging to the learning environment. It is perhaps in the first place necessary to consider the broadness, complexity and unpredictability of learning. At the theoretical/conceptual level, Greeno, Collins and Resnick note the complementarity of views on the nature of knowing, the nature of learning and transfer, and the nature of motivation and engagement offered by the behaviorist/empiricist, the cognitive/rationalist and the situative/pragmatist-sociohistoric perspectives.

Bandura's social learning theory stresses the observational nature of learning and thus the role of modelling of desirable and undesirable behaviors, an issue that has much relevance if one recognizes how much learning occurs almost 'incidentally', by being part of the community and media context. The case for real-world based learning is made by many authors have raised awareness about the thinness of learning processes that are mainly based on the recognition of but a small slice of a wide spectrum of intelligences. Yet others note the limitations inherent in the prevailing view that cognitive and meta-cognitive development terminate in early adulthood, an assumption which urgently needs to be reviewed in the light of research on life-span development.

Perrin refers to the non-traditional learner as the biggest untapped market for education. He quotes in that connection Hansen, Silver and Strong whose 'Learning Styles Inventory" identifies four different learning styles, i.e. directive, interactive, inquiry based, and creative. Most of what goes on in the educational establishment favors learners with a directive learning style and encourages the development of teachers and teaching styles that are effective for such learners. Yet others, like Burnett refer to the ephemeral and unpredictable nature of learning. However much we plan, or forget to plan, in the final analysis it is the learner who decides to derive from the learning environment what suits her or him best. In exploring to move from where we are to where we want to get, by moving away from an environment that was constructed out of a concern to deliver effectively fixed-modality instructional options to one that is oriented towards the demands of a multiplicity of learners and their varied range of goals and circumstances, one needs to have an open eye for opportunities. A willingness is required to look around for those instances where the current reality starts transforming itself into something new, as some of the cases referred to in this paper will highlight.

Policy Considerations

Policies can shape agendas, remove as well as create opportunities and barriers, legitimize or de-legitimize institutions, and define courses of action which will affect large numbers of people. They are powerful mechanisms for facilitating, sustaining and preventing broad-based change. However, educational policy making efforts over the last 40 years have been largely ineffective throughout the world.

There exists today a profound crisis of legitimacy in the realm of educational policy making. This does not stem from not being able to get the policies "right" or weak implementation capacity, but rather, from a deeper struggle over discourse and power. "Discourses are not just about what can be said, and thought; but also about who can speak, when, where, and with what authority".

Constructed within the context of modern democratic systems and nation-state structures, educational policy making is subject to the larger problems, i.e. the breakdown of social contracts and relationships and partisan politics, that confront these institutions.

Most people around the world do not feel (either due to apathy or because of genuine powerlessness) that they can influence or shape policies at any level of society, particularly at the national, international and supranational levels. Leaders often appear to be guided by personal interests rather than broader public interests. Just as the concept of open learning communities challenges us to think about learning and learning systems differently, it also calls for us to engage in thinking about educational policy making differently - to question dominant discourses and power in meaningful ways.

Simply enacting policies on open learning communities using conventional assumptions, frameworks, processes, institutions, language, and relationships will not be a sufficient strategy for enabling or sustaining open learning communities.

It proposes that policies be developed to support the dynamic interactions that take place in the learning system ecology which is comprised of:

1) the larger environment that surrounds open learning communities
2) each individual open learning community
3) the individual learners who participate in learning.

Development of each open learning community is seen as being simultaneously influenced and defined by both its larger environment, its interaction with other learning communities, and by the learners who participate in it.

Driven primarily by external political (i.e. the legitimizing nature of education for politicians) and financial (i.e. the big business of education) considerations, the content and scope of education policies contradict much of what we know about the diversity of learning needs, learning styles and processes, and learner backgrounds. Gardner observes that "while educators have always noted differences among learners, they have been strongly inclined to believe that all students can learn in similar ways." The bulk of educational policies in place today tend to narrowly focus on the institution of schooling and are still driven by notions of human capital formation, transmission-based processes, and mainstreaming learners into rigid tracking systems.

There is a strong need to refocus educational policies to reflect new ideas about learners, learning processes, and learning systems. Land and Hannafin frame this challenge for those involved in making policies as follows: "The learner is viewed as an active constructor of knowledge; accordingly, a need for systems that empower learners through self-directed learning has emerged." In addition, educational policies fail to recognize the powerful, informal dynamic learning environments that exist and are continually emerging, largely because of the spread of various information and communication technologies, and the growth of informal networks. Burnett describes that "Educational institutions which used to have control over knowledge and over its dissemination now find themselves in mediatized environments where education [schooling] is simply one of many different cultural experiences."

Most ministries of education have failed to make clear policies in relation to various media such as newspapers, radio, television, and the Internet. In addition, traditionally grounded in the primacy of the nation-state, current educational policies fail to reflect the dual forces of globalization and localization which are sweeping across the world. This implies that learning communities are potentially much larger than boundaries of the nation state and at the same time are much smaller than these boundaries. Within the context of this discussion, several implications for future policy directions begin to emerge. Two important priorities for widening the scope and content of educational policies include:

(a) recognizing the diversity of learners and that learning processes must take place at both individual and organizational levels, and

(b) seeing learning as taking place within mediatized environments.

A heuristic framework comprised of three sets of policy objectives that advance these priorities is proposed below. This framework attempts to incorporate several elements through which learning is mediated - language, technology and tools, values, human relationships, and information and images. It is shaped by belief that rigid distinctions between formal, non-formal and informal learning experiences are becoming increasingly irrelevant.

The framework deliberately does not assign responsibilities to any specific institution as it tries to flexibly allow for the multiple roles that any institution must play e.g., a distance learning organization may simultaneously serve as an environment supporting several different learning communities, as an open learning community, and as an actor within a wider learning community. For the sake of illustration, sample policies from around the world are mentioned to elaborate on certain objectives. However, it should be clarified at the outset that there is no one "right" policy framework. It is important that the exact scope and content of a particular policy framework vary according to the specific situation.

- Promote greater diversity of learning communities. Policies, for example, are being developed to accommodate the home schooling movement in the United States. In many Islamic countries, policies have been developed to promote madrasahs as learning spaces;

- Create more flexible connections and pluralistic interactions between learning communities;
- Remove geo-political and spatial boundaries between learning communities. For example, the Socrates Program being supported by the European Union is developing a Europe Transfer Credit System to facilitate the unconstrained movement of learners across learning communities;
- Promote and value learning for a broad range of life activities;
- Encourage respect for diverse knowledge systems and languages. For example, the Department of Renewable Resources, Northwest Territories of Canada has established a Traditional Knowledge Policy which provides a set of guidelines for incorporating traditional knowledge in government decision making and programs. A key aspect of this policy is its acknowledgment of oral tradition as a reliable source of information about traditional knowledge;
- Develop "literate" environments. In this respect, the notion of literacy should be interpreted quite broadly beyond its typical functional definitions. Policies should seek not only to stimulate the provision and use of reading and writing materials e.g., through libraries and local newspapers, but also to facilitate the development of environments which encourage demand for music, art, sports, nature, etc. The environment is also critical to the idea of distributed intelligence. Perkins describes the linkages between thinking and remembering and the environment as follows: "The surround - the immediate physical, social and symbolic resources

outside the person - participates in cognition, not just as a source of input and receiver of output but as a vehicle of thought. The surround in a real sense does part of the thinking. . .The surround in a real sense holds part of the learning."

- Stimulate the development and use of technologies for learning purposes. This would involve policies for accessing technologies for learning purposes such as subsidies and tax exemptions for hardware, lower telecommunication tariffs, and free/reduced-rate satellite broadcasting time.
- Facilitate the responsible sharing of information, ideas and experiences, between learning communities. The free flow of information will require that existing policies related to copyright laws and intellectual property rights be reviewed. Policies should also be developed which dis-incentivize the spread of or warn of potentially socially harmful information, i.e. pornography, violence, drugs. In Canada, for example, a rating system has been developed for television programs to warn viewers about the content;
- Develop distributed networks rather than central source providers. Policies which support standards for open architecture and connectivity to distributed resources should be developed;
- Create new spaces for experimentation and systemic learning.
- Develop the learning community into an inclusive entity. In the Phillippines, as part of a movement towards inclusive education, efforts are being made to link special education and regular schools more

closely. Blended classrooms are being encouraged which mix learners with special educational needs to non-impaired students;

- Increase the permeability of the boundaries of the learning community. For example, the Rover Learning Business opens up the use of its employee development centers to dealers and key suppliers;
- Create continuous and flexible opportunities for learning any time and anywhere. In many communities linked to farming activities, policies have been instituted to allow for flexible scheduling of the school calendar year in accordance with crops;
- Removal of formal requirements to access learning communities;
- Build multichannel learning modalities;
- Regulate the selection and availability of instructional resources. For example, in the United States, institutions are being encouraged to develop their own electronic information access policies. These policies should state that only Web sites that have educational and instructional value will be accessible, and that negotiated standards will be applied to determine what these sites and applications are. The policies should also address the ethics of computer-based information access, including software piracy, unauthorized access and privacy and confidentiality.
- Enhance the social dynamics within a learning community by developing an atmosphere of trust and cooperation;
- Support collaborative and interactive learning across generational groups;

- Remove discriminatory biases related to race, ethnicity, gender, class, sexual orientation or age, that limit access to certain learning communities.
- Support the construction of local knowledge and the evolution of local knowledge systems;
- Encourage the institution to engage in organizational learning.
- Encourage learners to be actively involved in building the learning community. Land and Hannafin describe, "The learner does not merely respond to the system; rather, he or she is integral to it." Policies which support learners in producing local "content" and local learning materials should be encouraged;
- Support the diverse needs of learners, their individual learning styles and their ability to access and create different learning communities. Many interesting policies are being developed in the field of Special Needs' Education that recognize the continuum of learners with differing needs and abilities. For example, in Thailand, the Individualized Educational Program (IEP) for All is an individualized curriculum or learning program. A typical IEP contains background information on the child including a learning profile and long and short term goals prepared in consultation with the child's parents and representatives from related educational or health/rehabilitation services;
- Validate different types of learning and learning experiences. In some countries, policies are being developed to support the Recognition of Prior Learning methodology which accredits learners for

knowledge and skills that they might have acquired through informal means;

- Reduce barriers of age and circumstance (social/cultural conditions, financial constraints, individual constraints [psychological/physical]). For example, the Rover Learning Business has developed the Rover employee assisted learning (REAL) program which offers each associate $175 in tuition fees every year for lateral personal development in areas not specifically related to current job skills. Many aid programs have tried to reduce the opportunity costs to learning by developing policies which provide financial incentives to parents to send their children, particularly their girls, to school;
- Assist learners in developing positive attitudes and feelings of motivation toward learning. This would involve developing policies which provide health, nutritional and psycho-social support to learners. It would also involve creating culturally-appropriate counseling services;
- Encourage learners to develop their own learning projects and to build their own learning communities.

There is a tension between autonomy and integration of open learning communities. What if a learning community wishes to isolate itself in order to preserve its own autonomy? The controversy surrounding home schooling in the United States serves to illustrate this tension. On the flipside of it is the challenge of how to meaningfully integrate diverse learning communities. This question is further complicated by concerns over unequal power relations that may exist between learning communities. Another related issue revolves around the classic debate of who decides on the policies. Policies involving censorship, relevance of learning resources, and languages have been particularly sensitive to these concerns. A third issue involves how to support micro to macro level flows of policies. More specifically, how can individual learners and learning communities participate in macro level decisionmaking? The next section concerning the process and actors will try to address some of these concerns.

The policymaking process is about human and institutional relationships, self-interests, power, money, information, and survival, and for these reasons, it is fundamentally political and it is always changing. This section will focus on the processes and the actors of the policymaking process, emphasizing two important aspects: learning and participation. Policies must be conceptually owned and practiced by people throughout the system in order to become real. The process of educational policy making is extremely complex, filled with contradictions and uncertainties, and influenced by many dynamic and powerful forces. Traditional assumptions underlying educational policy formation have failed to reflect this.

Policy making was viewed as taking place within a closed system. It was believed that the process could be controlled and predicted using mechanistic procedures and centralized institutions. It was also assumed that policies could be standardized and transferred along a wide spectrum of beneficiary groups, disregarding the fact that people differ from one another and their circumstances also differ. There was little attempt to understand the political economy of a situation. This resulted in a linear model of policy formation that was based on an input-process-output-outcome policy cycle.

Such "stages" models have since been critiqued. Porter argues that "we should not assume that policy making is a highly coherent and rational process, with a beginning, a middle, and an end - that each part leads logically and inexorably to each succeeding part."

According to DAE, policy making is a messy, fluid process which cannot be reduced to a simple linear mode. Crouch et al. describe one incarnation of this messy process: "Policy change usually takes place in a crisis mode. Policy itself is often nothing but the accretion of responses to past crises and half-hearted attempts to implement donor recommendations, operationalize vague ideological concepts from other sectors, or copy reforms from other countries." Under such conditions, Crouch et al. see policymaking more as a negotiation/bargaining process which takes place in the setting of a policy marketplace. It is comprised of diverse, competing groups, each trying to preserve and further their own vested interests i.e., state-affiliated bureaucracies, certain industries, political parties, teachers' unions, international donors. Porter attempts to capture the processes with a multiple streams model. "There are three process streams through which participants affect agendas. People recognize problems, generate proposals for policy change, and engage in such political activities as pressure group lobbying and election campaigns".

The separate streams of problems, policies, and politics each have lives of their own and are developed according to the rationale of the institutions to which they are linked. Solutions, problems, ideas, people and choices are all mixed together. Alliances, preferences and perceptions of policy actors are continually changing. This discussion on the policy making process has several implications for developing policies for open learning communities.

First, it means that we must move away from models that view policies in terms of top-down governmental declarations that are "officialized" in documents such as reports of special national commissions; the country's educational plan; the Ministry of Education Acts, Orders or Circulars; and reports of international agencies. Change should no longer be viewed solely as being centrally stimulated. We should see multiple policy processes in operation at institutional levels ranging from individual learning communities to local, district, regional, national, international, supranational groupings. Rather than being forced to adopt policy blueprints, each of these institutional formations should be encouraged to initiate and develop their own policies on learning. This requires a different framework for thinking about who are policy makers, what their roles are, and what their area of jurisdiction is. The role of educational policymaking should no longer be the sole domain of sectoral ministries. Institutions concerned with supporting learning, whether they be schools, NGOs, media groups, distance learning providers, etc. must increasingly see themselves as important policymaking entities. Policy processes must be continually concerned with creating spaces for allowing alternative voices to be heard.

Second, policy formulation and implementation should not be viewed as discrete activities but rather as a continuous learning and experimentation effort. Rather than looking at policies from a fixed-state point of view, we may wish to conceive of a system of rolling policies which are continually monitored, reflected upon, discussed and appropriately modified as time progresses.

Policy processes must play a dual role of implementing a vision as well as continually creating the vision. Underlying this policy learning system should be a strong emphasis on active, ongoing policy learning by organizational entities at different levels, including the citizenry at large, who are involved in the process. Such a system should be supported by data, analysis and dialogue. To make this exercise meaningful, however, would imply some dramatic changes in these tools. Data on learning would have to move beyond simply looking at the formal sector. If policy makers really want to understand what is going on in a learning system, they will need not only a comprehensive system of indicators but a full research portfolio which is capable of looking at mediatized environments, information networks and the diversity of learners and learning processes. Analytical tools must also be reworked to take into account more dynamic multidisciplinary relationships and to discourage the tendency to settle for first-order solutions. These should be geared towards continually raising difficult questions rather than providing quick-fix answers.

Dialogue is probably the most critical of these three elements and is the one requiring the most change as it fundamentally relates to issues of participation. Botkin, Elmandjra, and Malitza describe the traditional thinking that guides dialogue. "The conventional, often unarticulated, conception of how societies learn usually starts with one or more centers of concentrated competence as the emanaters of new discoveries, theories, beliefs and solutions. These new ideas are then disseminated to larger circles of people and the public at large.

The role of society at large is reduced to adjusting to and consuming the discoveries and knowledge produced at centers of expertise". Crouch elaborates on this by describing his model of policy dialogue as a process of marketing. "To put it crudely, policy dialogue is a highly sophisticated, carefully crafted sales process that creates the feeling of inclusiveness and co-ownership of reform. The important goal is to create ownership of the decisions after the fact" . Such models of only involving stakeholders in information sharing and consultation and excluding them from the initiation and conceptualization represent a dangerous form of manipulation and must be strongly challenged. Participation must go beyond mere invitations to accept given solutions or ingenious attempts to capture goodwill and support for given products. Participation is not simply about expanding the range of stakeholders; rather, it should be geared around encouraging participatory conceptualization.

Third, we must try to introduce more flexibility into the process. Policy development is a continuous process that should not be circumscribed by artificial political or operational time frames or fiscal years. Part of the challenge is also identifying the right timing (i.e., windows of opportunity) for catalyzing policy change processes. This may require the development of special policies that support an ongoing process of identifying opportunities. Benveniste describes that we need policies that continually allow us to find out that change is needed. He says that we need policies that allow us to bend existing rules. There is also need for temporary authority structures that allow us to experiment and modify what we are doing. Such structures should be comprised as intersectoral work teams. Organizational learning also requires a different framework of incentives. In order to seize opportunities and learn, we often have to take risks, make errors, and correct them. Few organizations currently reward those who take risks and make mistakes. Many policies, in fact, encourage people to hide mistakes or, worse, to remain inactive.

Fourth, it is also important to encourage the continuity of actors who are involved. Effective dialogue is premised on trust, understanding and a willingness to compromise, which can only happen when actors know each other. Continuity is also particularly important for building up an institutional memory. Many things go unwritten or are understood in the policy formation process.

Opening up the policy process fundamentally involves redistributing and sharing power, which is itself a messy process and will make many people uncomfortable. In addition, supporting a good process is expensive and will require significant budgetary shifts. However, if learning and social justice is a priority for humanity, then we must push strongly for spending more than 4% of the global government budget on learning. We can also expect significant resistance from people who continue to focus on yesterday's solutions and are unwilling to look towards the future. Under such resistance, facilitating a shift in policy direction will require a new type of commitment from all of us. "Establishing policies and programs to enhance innovative learning are dependent on at least one premise: a willingness to initiate fundamental processes of change, even when all of their implications are not known with total certainty in advance". This requires that we are willing to question our own privileged roles as "experts" and "authorities." It also means that we must see ourselves as learners - building a vision, not simply implementing one.

Many positive experiences have taken place with new opportunities emerging every day. Many changes are already dynamically taking place. Our task must then start with continually linking these experiences into a coherent vision and building a critical mass of partners around the world. We must also focus on developing more robust frameworks and methodologies that both integrate our understanding about learners and learning processes and complex systems, and allow us to continually see new realities.

Open Learning In Developing Countries

The spread of information and communication technology is helping many of us envision the practical potential and possibly inevitable proliferation of open learning environments to address all kinds of learning needs in all parts of the world. Although the proliferation of opportunities for open learning will accelerate in the years ahead, they will not replace schools, particularly for children and adolescents and most certainly not in developing countries. The frontiers of the school wall provide security for the young and peace of mind for their parents. Schools provide important socialization functions.

Developing countries have invested heavily in the universalization of primary schools, and there is good evidence that attending school has many social and private benefits - especially for girls. However imperfect schools are as environments for learning, they will be with us long into the future. We believe that primary and secondary schools in developing countries can be assisted to provide more open learning environments. We believe that "openness" can be achieved in a kind of four-dimensional framework. These dimensions are not distinct categories, and development activities may be located in one or more dimensions at the same time. The four dimensions are as follows:

- opening the environment to improve educational quality;
- opening the environment to enhance access/equity;
- opening the environment to expand the range of resources for learning;
- opening the environment to provide stronger learner control and linkages for learning.

Opening the environment to improve educational quality: Visits to schools in developing countries show that learning environments are typically ones where teachers and students are locked into interactions that are not conducive to effective learning. The dynamics of the teaching-learning process are marked by strategies that view students as passive recipients of poorly organized and de-contextualized pieces of curricular information.

Educational objectives, to the extent they are explicit, tend to call for getting students to memorize this information, and the road to memorization is having students pronounce correctly, repeat, or copy the information given. It is infrequent to find students being asked to interpret information, to think critically or creatively, to predict or elaborate, to solve a problem, or to engage in any number of activities to assist students in making meaning of the information before them.

The orienting stimuli in the instructional process are usually boring and devoid of relevance to the lives of students. As a result, there is little engagement in the learning process. The quality of education, judged against almost any definition, is low. One of the most successful approaches to improving educational quality in the face of conditions encountered in schools in developing countries is that of interactive radio instruction (IRI). IRI is a methodology that has evolved through twenty years of experience in more than a dozen countries. It differs significantly from other forms of radio instruction because

(a) radio plays a primary rather than supplementary instructional role and

(b) lessons are designed to follow proven principles of learning, are subjected to systematic formative evaluation, and are developed to engage learners in active learning.

Interactive radio instruction audio programmes are delivered by radio or cassettes with accompanying printed materials. Interactive radio instruction has shown that it consistently and significantly influences learners' performance in a variety of educational subjects.

During the past twenty years, interactive radio instruction has been used to teach mathematics, language, science, health, environmental studies, civic education, child development, and adult basic education. Interactive radio lessons to teach English developed recently in the Republic of South Africa are now being broadcast nationally, and efforts are underway to use IRI to teach mathematics in that country.

Opening the environment to improve access/equity: The second dimension in making learning more open has to do with access/equity. Too often, various factors impinge on a young person's chances to attend school. Especially affected are those who must work for a living, persons living in remote or underpopulated communities, girls, and various ethnic groups. It is often the case that distances to schools are too long, the school schedule is incompatible with work at home or a job, or other constraints make it difficult to attend regular school programs.

Developing countries are showing greater interest in exploring distance education methods to reach these groups of learners. There are also instances where distance is not an issue and school facilities may be opened in such a way as to permit greater access/equity for those unable to attend regular school programs. This kind of openness will be especially important for countries hoping to expand the cycle of basic education to include junior secondary education. There is a number of examples of attempts to open up secondary education by establishing study centers or making alternative use of existing facilities. A particularly interesting example is Indonesia's SMP Terbuka. This model makes possible junior secondary education for students who would not otherwise take part because of geographic or socio-economic obstacles. Students are attached to study centers near their homes, which are linked to a nearby secondary school. Students engage in self-study and group learning, interact with teacher aides, and receive occasional face-to-face instruction from teachers at the nearby secondary school. There is flexibility built into scheduling to make it possible for young people who work to attend school. The SMP Terbuka model provides a good example of how greater access to education may be achieved by a strategy that opens the use of existing resources to new educational purposes.

Opening the environment to expand the range of resources for learning: There is much that schools in developing countries can do to open their windows to the world - to enrich the learning process by going beyond the resources for learning that are typically available in the classroom. We see striking examples of learners in schools throughout the world making use of the Internet and other electronic networks to connect to sources of information not available in the classroom or to work collaboratively in joint projects or information exchange with learners in other schools. Such activities are excellent routes to developing communication, information gathering, and problem solving skills and providing practice in dealing with multiple perspectives. Computers and electronic connections from schools in developing countries to outside resources are likely to become more common in the future.

Already some developing countries - Chile is a good example - are making good use of computers to enrich learning. For the near future, access to computers in schools will remain out of reach for many. But there are possibilities for opening and enriching the learning process through a wider range of learning resources that are available to schools in poor communities. Adoption of "best practices" for teaching and learning will make learning environments more receptive to strategies and resources that go beyond the lecture/recitation/seatwork paradigm that characterizes so much of traditional teaching in schools.

The benefits of inquiry, discovery, and group projects need not involve electronic mediation or expensive resources - they can be achieved through thoughtful organization and resources that can be found in the community. Students in Costa Rica, for example, learned much about science, the environment, and the local economy by getting outside the classroom and tapping the knowledge of community members. Similarly, in schools where reading materials are scarce, effective learning materials may be generated that draw upon the experience of students and their parents. "Experience stories" are part of best practice even in schools where reading materials are abundant.

Opening The Environment To Provide Stronger Learner Control And Linkages For Learning: An important dimension of openness in learning environments that is achievable by schools in developing countries right now has to do with affording learners stronger control and linkages for learning. What this involves is ensuring that students are provided the opportunities for learning in such a way that it will assist them to function as well as they can as lifelong learners when they leave school. Unfortunately, most schools in developing countries do not have this as a goal. Education is seen as years in school, with content broken up into bits to be hammered by teachers into students for demonstration on examinations. As a result, students leave school having had few chances to develop a meta-cognitive awareness of how to direct their own learning as they approach the challenges of work and daily life. Few have had the opportunity of learning in group-supported rather than solitary endeavor. Few have had the opportunities to make even the most basic choices of what to learn or how to learn it. Most have memorized (and probably forgotten) facts about democracy; few have had the opportunity to practice it. This kind of opening of the learning environment can occur through a commitment to best practice that can be found throughout the world. Colombia's Escuela Nueva provides a good example of how schools may contribute to a greater participation of students in the management of the schools. Such opportunities to practice and observe democracy and engage in "real time" problem solving will strengthen the chances for students to become active and effective life-long learners.

Problems of social change in South Africa have little precedence elsewhere, given the acutely skewed politicized nature of policy and provisioning over some 50 years of minority privileged rule. With the advent of a democratic dispensation committed to the institution and consolidation of a system of greater equity and access in all of its sectors, the degree of energy and optimism required needs little elaboration here. Suffice it to say, the awesome challenges confronting the new incumbents to office staggering though they might be, are being engaged with the vigour and tenacity they warrant.

This scenario, though commonplace within all social sectors, is perhaps nowhere more pressing than in that most contested terrain subject to turmoil since 1976, and consequently representing the test bed for political emancipation - the educational sector. Gross disparities in educational provisioning for black and white South Africans until recently, were rightfully perceived as the hallmark of a blatantly discriminatory and iniquitous order.

Engineering of educational policy along the lines of ethnicity and language within the 'homelands', was preceded by a rash proliferation of disparate, unwieldy and poorly managed educational authorities, tasked with providing 'education for disempowerment' for the vast majority of the population. Little room existed for discourse on issues of relevance, curriculum, language, teacher capacity and schools' effectiveness, much less contemporary trends and practices. South African educational practice, insulated from contemporary developments, was effectively rendered irrelevant to the majority of those it was ostensibly designed for, inherently behaviorist in practice, content and methodology. Unfettered subscription to rote, repetition and regurgitative methodologies, antagonistic to more enlightened teaching approaches, comprised the mainstay of methodology and paradigm.

The present Herculean challenges to educational reconstruction, are in no small measure commensurable with the dysfunctionality of previous structural design. Much of this is now conventional wisdom. Perhaps more important, are the implications for present capacity to transform the system in the context of a renewal of culture and ethos within education, at the dawn of the new millennium. Peculiar though its problems might be, South Africa would not be the first country experiencing the imperative of systemic educational transformation. Many African countries embarked upon similar policies in the wave and wake of independence in the post war period.

Observations of transformation dialectics in several developing countries might prove instructive and offer leads as to where and when 'turning points' have been reached, in the protracted and often obfuscating change process. However, the present status of education and available capacities within this and other critical sectors, urge the examination of a few observations and issues potentially impacting upon medium and longer term national transformation goals. The Department of National Education places considerable store by such central concerns as equity of access, universality, quality, rehabilitation, democracy and diversity within education, accountability, and open and lifelong learning, etc. Whilst these and the many other goals that might be included, each warrant meticulous attention in that they constitute the under girds to educational reconstruction, all of these aspects will not be discussed here, for reasons of space.

However, four essential areas are singled out for discussion in the context of how these are given application within the work of NGOs in general, and that of OLSET, the Open Learning Systems Education Trust, more specifically. These respective strands are neither hierarchically ranked nor necessarily separate and disjointed, rather they resonate more sharply with the outcomes based activities within the microcosm of the educational renewal project alluded to. The four areas are:

- Teacher capacity development and related inservicing (INSET) programmes
- Curriculum reform and outcomes based objectives
- Equity of access and quality of instruction
- Transformation management capacity for expediting open learning environments.

Teacher capacity development and INSET: The Open Learning Systems Education Trust, a non-governmental organization formed in the heady days of imminent change in South Africa, represented local efforts at employing Interactive Radio Instruction (IRI) as a means to affording Junior Primary Teachers in under-resourced and remote rural schools, concretized classroom based support and teaching strategies tantamount to a shift in daily classroom practice. In the context of an inordinately high over representation of Junior Primary teachers in the un- and under qualified categories, OLSET's IRI initiative focused upon three critical and high failure areas for the black learners, English Language, Mathematics and Science. To date, English Language and Mathematics programmes have been developed, the latter not beyond the pilot stage.

A low threat intervention, Radio Learning serves as an appropriate technology vehicle for shifting orthodox pre servicing methodologies to more relevant approaches in keeping with the demands of a new educational dispensation. OLSET's teaching methodology, premised upon the new national curriculum, aimed at innovative learner centered approaches to improving instructional quality as well as teacher effectiveness in the classroom situation. Pupil teacher ratios remain high in schools throughout South Africa, a situation further impacting the already poor outcomes and high failure, repetition and drop-out rates. Admittedly, research findings indicate that class size might be overplayed in pointing to causality in failure rates. However, ratios as high as 120:1, as many OLSET schools attest to, cannot be entertained as having no bearing on quality of educational instruction.

Unlike several Latin American instances, South African Radio Learning does not represent a supplementary or enrichment strategy in introducing new curricular objectives. It constitutes a core curriculum alternative delivery and practice, where teachers are inadequately trained for effective teaching of communication skills, often in spite of the regulatory pre servicing period. Radio Learning in this instance, offers an invaluable entry point to teacher inservicing and support, regardless of distance from center. For many thousands of teachers, this radio access remains the sole significant professional contact with current mainstream developments in educational reconstruction. Given the embryonic status of the newly instituted provincial educational authorities, it is plausible that they would otherwise remain marginalized for a considerable time in the foreseeable future, in a country where some 60% of population still reside rurally.

Measurable gains are being attained by way of learner outcomes and teacher upgrading via inservicing strategies such as Teacher Support Group mechanisms and daily classroom lesson observation and monitoring. Elaborate but uncomplicated user friendly Teacher Guides outlining daily radio program content, aims and objectives, serve as an indispensable guide to all project teachers and necessarily their unqualified peers, more so. Extra mural Teacher Development modules by radio/ audio, are seen as potentially powerful inservicing modalities, with work already in progress. The impact of such strategies on development might ultimately depend on the extent to which they are employed in conjunction with other systemic strategies in the provinces. Positive evaluation findings regarding the IRI initiative in seven of South Africa's nine provinces, continue to inform and encourage further work and innovation within the field of distance education by radio. It is clear that the open learning modalities of IRI in South Africa, especially in Teacher Upgrading and Inservicing, have yet to be exploited to their full potential. Such an approach could effectively link levels of capacity and learning and enable learners to move to higher skills levels, from any starting point. An open learning strategy of this sort, might prove a timely and immensely powerful channel for educational skills development and enhancement.

Curriculum reform constitutes the central plank to educational reconstruction in South Africa. The 'what' and 'how' of the new national curriculum underpins the quality of education in the new dispensation. Issues of language, methodology, cultural relevance and assessment instruments, have not in the past been seen as pertinent issues within the provisioning structures. In the massification of education where mainstreaming will take precedence over other concerns, tensions between social and individual needs cannot be ignored without potentially negative consequences.

Historical disparities have resulted in a backdrop of uneven and disparate achievements within and between constituencies nation-wide. The temptation to standardize curricula at the expense of client orientated education demand, such as in the 'northern suburb syndrome' (formerly all white, but increasingly black middle class schools) where educational resources are comparable with developed country status, presents difficult tensions for newly empowered decision makers. Primary concerns lie with mainstreaming of previously marginalized communities and as such preclude needs of the well heeled educational sector.

Distance education and open learning models are gaining increasing currency as equally effective alternative provisioning systems for the better placed as well as severely deprived educational constituencies. Innovative curricula using media such as radio integrated with print materials, are considered cost-effective quality options. More notably, curriculum reform demonstrates cognizance of skills needs, trends and concerns likely to be commonplace in the new information technology century. Distance education combined with conventional classroom modalities, is becoming standard practice even in rural settings, surely an encouraging sign of comfort levels with multichannel applications, however low tech and off the beaten information highway it may be.

A recently published audit characterizes South Africa's 360 000 teachers, as 'all being in need of some form of inservice training - INSET.' The implications of this professional deficit for curricular changes and paradigm shift, are staggering. Seen in another light, this might constitute immense opportunities for relevant upgrading and repositioning of teacher skills in tune with the information driven needs of the rapidly evolving teaching ecosystem of the imminent 21st century. What is essentially considered a disturbingly acute deficit of teacher capacity presently, could be used to great advantage if perceived for the implicit opportunity it offers on the eve of a world-wide paradigm shift in education provisioning and the new skills versatility required of teachers in fast evolving economies.

The system must increasingly open access to education and training opportunity to all children, youth and adults, and provide a means for learners to move easily from one context to another, so that the possibilities of lifelong learning are enhanced..... Levelling the playing fields in education and training, so that the States resources are used to provide the same quality of education to all... Equity and access must be linked to quality improvement of education and training services..."

That Radio Learning already offers daily access to all but two provinces of South Africa's nine provinces in a relatively short period of development, is not fortuitous. Daily rural outreach is unsustainable by most other means, given the expanse and isolated nature of rural communities. In anticipation of this provisioning concern, OLSET embarked upon an instructional design, portable across the provinces in terms of content, curricular approaches and methodology, easily accessible by the prevalence of radios in most communities in the country.

Access issues, however, have not been narrowly confined to 'availability on the air'. Acknowledgement of various learning styles and media preferences within the radio instructional design (all not being able to be accommodated of necessity) imputes more generous construction consensus around the notion of equity of access. Learners are offered an array of approaches to lesson content and structures, in order to accommodate learning style preferences as much as possible. Story, song, motion, music, rhyme, peer teaching, print and graphics, radio, teacher interaction, face to face, total physical engagement, etc., are deployed in imaginative combinations encouraging greater active participation in the learning process. Evaluations show several aspects of learner performances have been impacted positively, and 'equity of access' of content by considerably more pupils within the learning situation, is seen as contra distinct to 'as many as possible accessing the program.'

Similarly, teacher development and inservicing by radio, print and audio and face-to-face combinations, are perceived as potential viable routes to open learning configurations, whereby access is addressed meaningfully through voluntary entry and exit points and not solely through physical outreach connotations.

"Government's commitment to reconstruction and development of the education system as a whole" implies a total overhaul of the educational system. Commitment to systemic change is synonymous with change of conventional delivery in education, methodological paradigms, teacher practices, learning and teaching approaches, accreditation, critical thinking skills, generation, pedagogical skills, and the development and consolidation of open learning environments. In formulating the framework for so enormous a task at national and provincial levels, consideration must be given to the availability of capacity to manage and oversee this complex and protracted process. South Africa is perhaps the last country on the continent to embrace transformation late in the century, and as such, might look to the lessons and fortunes of its neighbours as well as further afield, in its challenging path of transformation.

Providing opportunities to meet Africa's basic learning needs is a first step towards a long-term solution to prepare the Continent for its future in a global society. Africa's example has taught us that these learning needs cannot be addressed only by expanding the formal education system, but require new ways to look at both access to and quality of education and learning. National policies in Africa are placing a high priority on improving education, for example through initiating curriculum reforms, improving in-service teacher training and reinforcing non-formal and distance education approaches. Teacher training colleges, working with the relevant departments within Ministries of Education, have been major partners in implementing such new directions and programmes. Their role in improving the quality of learning could be extended beyond the traditional training of teachers by their becoming:

1. an information, communication and learning resource for educational planners and researchers,

for teachers and, through them, for specific learning communities, and

2. a test bed for innovation in teaching and learning. Advances in information and communication technologies (ICT) can facilitate such processes, if applications take full account of technical constraints and educational concepts.

In the eighties, Africa had the highest growth figures in educational enrolment at all levels as well as in expenditure on education (as a percentage of GNP). In the nineties, these figures have stagnated or even declined, leaving Africa with more than 200 million illiterate adults (44% of the adult population) gross enrolment figures in sub-Saharan Africa at 73,1 %, 23.1 %, and 3,3 % at primary, secondary and tertiary level respectively, and alarmingly high unemployment figures among educated youth. Africa's example shows us that an enormous expansion of the formal education system alone cannot address existing, let alone future, basic learning needs, and even adds new sets of problems such as increased need for training and re-training of teachers, for adaptation of curricula, more textbooks and learning materials, and for improved communications and administration systems.

Different patterns of labour, new ideas on political participation and human rights, multi-cultural societies, and environmental problems are evolving in Africa, as elsewhere. Pressures of the contemporary age require people and institutions to continuously acquire new knowledge and skills. Today's globalization of the economy and international trade have made education a crucial element of socio-economic development. Learning is no longer an initial activity preparing one for a productive life, but rather a continuous necessity to cope with societies' changing demands. This increased need for lifelong learning opportunities takes on a special meaning in the African context, presenting not only a challenge to the limited effectiveness of the traditional school systems in meeting basic learning needs, but also a historic opportunity to leap-frog into the Information Age to participate and compete as equal partners in our global society.

At the World Conference on Education for All the leaders of the world adopted an "expanded" vision of basic education, that surpasses present resource levels, institutional structure, curricula and conventional delivery systems. UNESCO has responded to this challenge by creating the Learning Without Frontiers Programme that aims to promote diversified and open learning systems in the perspective of lifelong learning, emphasising the potential contribution of modern information and communication technologies (ICTs) to create more meaningful and open learning environments.

Internet connectivity on the African continent lags far behind that of the rest of the world. Although rapid progress this year will fully connect all but one of the capitals of African countries to the Internet. Where full Internet access exists, it is generally restricted to the largest cities and its cost is far beyond the means of public sector users. At the same time, more and more countries are also providing full access to remote areas, and prices are seen to drop significantly over time. However, still about 70% of African's population does not live in reach of Internet access points. Both inadequate telecommunications systems, the socio-economic situation, as well as lack of human resources in some countries are the main reason for Africa's low connectivity.

Technical roadblocks are also important in efforts to stimulate access to the information highway for development in Africa at both the national and individual levels. Five of the major ones in many African countries are:

1. the small number of potential users having both the skills and equipment to benefit from access to electronic information networks;
2. the scarcity and high costs of equipment, software and information compared to situations in the North;
3. lack of reliable and accessible physical telecommunications infrastructure;
4. telecommunications monopoly, associated with overly restrictive regulations and high costs, and
5. lack of interregional networking and cooperation.

Currently several initiatives are under way to improve connectivity and networking on the African continent. At the basic infrastructure level, two of the major initiatives are Rascom, the Regional African Satellite Communications Organisation that aims to carry all satellite traffic within Africa through the co-ordination of satellite capacity, and Africa One, an AT&T project to lay optical fibre cable around the continent with gateways to all the coastal countries interested.

In the area of capacity building and policy making reference should be made to the Africa's Information Society Initiative (AISI), an action framework approved by the Economic Commission for Africa (ECA)

Conference of Ministers in May 1996 to build Africa's information and communication infrastructure and to promote national development and regional integration through telematics applications in priority areas such as finance, employment, tourism, health and education. A recent overview by Mike Jensen provides a more comprehensive view on connectivity in Africa.

Information and communication technologies, and in particular telematics applications, dramatically expand the options for engaging in teaching and learning at individual, community and societal levels, especially for those who have not been able to obtain an education, due to inadequate numbers of schools and qualified teachers in particular, or to barriers such as inadequate time schedules, age limitations, educational fees, or language of instruction.

ICTs provide opportunities for greater flexibility, interactivity and accessibility through multi-channel applications such as interactive radio and television, video conferencing, teletext, Internet based virtual communities (ranging from the chatroom to academic discussion circles), WWW publishing and individualised CD-ROM tutorials which can support both classroom teaching and learning in a distance education mode.

ICTs can connect schools, universities and research centres and libraries in order to promote and support collaboration among students, teachers and research sources, and reduce communications and administrative costs through networks linking educational establishments and governmental bodies. Through ICTs, learning opportunities can be made available to the community on a 24-hour basis, thereby establishing an important condition for an open learning environment.

However, in the educational context, it must be remembered that ICTs are simply tools for facilitating learning and teaching. Their success does not depend on the technology itself, but on the appropriateness of its application.

High expectations for ICT applications may cause disappointment among their users, if they do not take full account of the actual educational contexts including, for example, untrained users, unreliable supply of electricity, and, more importantly, educational messages that do not meet the standards of quality and relevance.

Despite considerable effort at educational reform, Africa, seen at a large scale, has been unable to adequately meet the essential learning needs of its communities. Compounding immense problems of infrastructure, human and financial resources and organisation, and perhaps even more important for the fundamental basis of education in Africa are:

i) lack of access to needed information and learning resources to enhance Africa's capacity to improve existing formal education systems, and

ii) lack of communication among key players in the learning process: students and their parents, educators, researchers and education officials (planners, policy makers and curriculum developers) which has often resulted in a bureaucratic and top-down approach to the provision of learning opportunities.

In many African countries, teacher training colleges (TTCs) are instrumental in the implementation of educational changes through pre- and in-service training programmes. However, they could play a much more prominent role in creating learning environments that are responsive to the specific needs of communities through:

i) establishing communication among teacher educators and teachers and, through them students, parents, and also Ministries of Education to interact with policy makers and central support services on actual learning needs and limitations of current educational directions, and

ii) creating learning resource centres to support both professional capacity building of teacher educators and (trainee) teachers and the development of relevant learning activities.

As part of the National Information and Communication Infrastructures (NICI), being prepared in the framework of the larger: "Harnessing Information Technology for Development in Africa" project, a maximum of four teacher training colleges (TTCs) in each of the twenty African countries will be provided with full access to the Internet. The teacher training colleges will be encouraged through this access to:

1. establish dialogue with educational planners and policy makers, researchers and practising teachers to ensure a more meaningful development and implementation of directives and regulations;

2. exploit information on latest concepts, developments and experiments to support professional development;

3. develop relevant curricula through groupwork and groupware, in close collaboration with the relevant national education authorities;

4. develop appropriate teaching and learning materials, using locally relevant images and sounds;

5. apply the Internet as a tool to address the needs of different learner groups.

The participating countries will be selected on the basis of national commitment and availability of sufficient infrastructure and connectivity to support the proposed learning networks. The implementation of the different project activities in the twenty participating countries will be monitored, evaluated and assessed through discussions and exchange of experience at the regional and international levels.

Constrains of the Internet for Education

The history of Education cannot be told apart from its technology. From orality to literacy, from manuscripts to the printed page, from text to hypertext, the prevailing technologies supporting education have defined its very nature. Stopping short of technological determinism, we acknowledge the chicken-and-egg relationship between technology, education, and society. The possibilities which education brings to society depend upon the affordances of the undergirding technology. We use the term affordance to describe a potential for action, the perceived capacity of an object to enable the assertive will of the actor.

There are many objects in our environment. Some we ignore, some we adapt to, and some we appropriate for our assertive will. It is the objects in this last category which fall under the the definition of affordances. Certain objects afford opportunities for action. An affordance is a value-rich ecological object that is understood by direct perception. Perception informs the individual of affordances. Action transforms affordances into effectivities which extend human capabilities. Our own bodies are affordances. The eyes afford perception, the ears listening, the hands manipulation, the tongue and vocal cords afford utterances.

Natural affordances emerge into effectivities through use in conscious activity. The hand of an infant, though attached, is a separate object. The infant is amused by it, studies it, tastes it, touches other things with it. Soon the infant learns to use the hand to manipulate other objects. In the process, the hand gradually transforms its object-ness to subject-ness. The child becomes less conscious of the hand as she uses it as an extension of her own intentioned will. The affordance becomes an effectivity. Technology and media are affordances to the extent that they promise extended human capabilities of seeing, hearing, and uttering.

Tools are affordances to the extent they offer extended human capabilities for manipulating things in the environment. Through use, skill is acquired and the object becomes an extension of ourselves. These artifacts are transformed from affordances to effectivities.

Five thousand years ago the affordances of orality and rhetoric were extended by the technology of written text. Writing enabled the precision of recorded memory. It afforded cognitive communication across time and distance. Literacy gave birth to History. The written word introduced constraints of grammar and syntax, but out of these constraints emerged stability and permanence of language. It was a means of representing and archiving human knowledge for later retrieval by one's self or by another. We look at antiquity through the eyes of those who could read and write, shading, perhaps, our view of the importance of literacy in shaping history. When we think of antiquity, Athens invariably comes to mind. Athens was among the few ancient cultures that valued literacy. Athens provided a system of public education which included reading and writing, an affordance we take for granted today. But, just as it is today, not all Athenians chose to appropriate skills of literacy. Athens produced history's most famous illiterate, Socrates, who opposed the technology of writing on the grounds that it would corrupt the human mind and destroy the memory of mankind.

We suggest, from the standpoint of affordance, that Socrates perceived no need to write. After all, he had his graduate students, Xenophon and Plato, to record his words for him. But more fundamentally the assertive will of Socrates found its full potential within the affordance of oral discourse and dialog. Indeed, for most of written history, writing was not an affordance for the common person. For centuries, it was the exclusive realm of the power elite. The manuscript was an instrument of power. The written word is a permanent record, an objective archive, a sense of authority. Manuscripts were guarded, protected and generally inaccessible. For thousands of years, written knowledge was the affordance of the literate few: the priests and princes who controlled access to manuscripts and who had the skills to make use of the technology. Those who controlled knowledge controlled the collective conscience, the laws, the social structures, and the tax records. Literacy was the means of social control.

In the period approaching the late middle ages, the power of literacy began to spread to the merchant class. Universities emerged in the thirteenth century, before the age of Gutenberg. Manuscripts were extremely costly, reproduction of a single copy required weeks of labor by an established member of the literati. Often, students copied their own texts, transcribing oral recitations by a lecturer/reader. Learning to read and write was the privilege of an elite few. For those without means, a literate education was characterized by extreme effort supported only by primitive techniques and rudimentary tools.

Entry into the literate community was not possible without great personal sacrifice. Manuscripts, the objects that enabled this intention, were affordances for acquiring literacy. The rise of the universities in Europe and the neo-classicism associated with the return of the Crusaders in the thirteenth century drove unprecedented demands on manuscript production. In a previous era, this renaissance would die before it began, lacking the infrastructure to support the propagation of knowledge. But modern technology was on the horizon.

The mid fifteenth century saw the convergence of several unrelated developments: the wine press, paper production, oil-based ink, block printing, and finally, movable type. The modern age arrived with the first edition of Gutenberg's Bible. The cost of book production fell by several hundred fold. A printer could reproduce a thousand copies of a book in the time it took a scribe to reproduce four copies of the same text. Within a few years there were more circulated copies of Scripture and the major classics than had existed previously for all time. In the coming years, the Scriptures and the classics became affordances, not for spiritual ends, but as a means of learning how to read and write, as a means of mastering reason, logic and rhetoric. The affordance of archived knowledge burst free from the constrictive grip of monks, priests and courtiers.

The power of print technology was in the hands of an emerging ruling class. The printing press was an affordance for Martin Luther to assert his Ninety-five Theses, challenging established authority. The emerging years brought the Reformation, the Enlightenment and democracy. The bourgeois state triumphed over monarchies. Liberalism instituted basic rights and freedoms: The rights of private property, freedom of self-expression, and freedom of the press. These "self-evident" rights spread throughout the Western world. They were the expressed freedoms for all citizens, but they were particular effectivities for those who owned property, those who possessed the skills associated with self expression, and those who owned or controlled the presses. The modern age became an age of reading and writing (mostly reading). Book learning changed the nature of basic education throughout the West.

The providers of education (initially the church, and ultimately the state) perceived it as an institutional affordance to foster morality, patriotism and citizenship. Education itself was primarily moral (the intention of the institution) and secondarily intellectual (the intention of the learner). Educational technologies (the textbooks, the lessons, the methods) were designed to carry out the primary intention. The Massachusetts law of 1647 made its intentions explicit: to disable the "project of that old deluder Satan to keep men from the knowledge of the Scriptures". Doctrinal intentions prevailed for over two hundred years in American Schools. Instructional technology reflected those intentions. The hornbook was designed to teach basic reading, but more importantly, Christian doctrine. This technology was a wooden frame on a handle. The frame enclosed a single printed page containing the English alphabet followed by the text of the Lord's Prayer.

From 1836 to 1907 the McGuffy Readers set the standard for American grammar school education. There is rarely a page in that series of six readers which does not address itself to some moral problem from the standpoint of Protestant Christianity and Victorian ethics. The six books propagated a middle-class, conventional, paternalistic morality, reflecting the values of the dominant culture. Education molded the collective conscience.

Education in the twentieth century retains a content-centered paradigm of institutional affordance. However, this has been a century of major curricular reforms. The changes have reflected a more diverse and complex society with a broader range of values and priorities. As our society continues to diversify, as the need for technical skill increases, as the world changes faster than textbooks and lesson plans can keep pace, the emphasis on curriculum content is giving way to a focus on the learning process.

Constructivism, considered radicalism a decade ago, is the dominant perspective at most educational conferences. Content objectives are giving way to a focus on skills development, instructional designs are giving way to learning environments where students define the central tasks, including how the learning should be monitored, assessed and adjusted to achieve the desired outcomes. Such strategies bring flexibility to the educational process, adjusting to continued change in a postmodern world.

Today's information technology enables the transition from modern to postmodern, no less than the printing press enabled the transition from pre-modern. Technology has changed the way we consider content. In a 14th century university classroom, a manuscript of Rhetoric was likely the exclusive source of information. That was a constraint imposed by the technology. Today, we can download Rhetoric in seconds, but we can also download related texts, commentaries, research studies, historical perspectives, ad infinitum. We can scan these texts with the eye of a computer, discovering patterns, linking them to allied texts, offering multiple dimensions of textual analysis.

Interactivity

In recent years, a prime objective in media development has been the quality of interactivity. This has been especially true with educational media, starting in the 1950s with Skinner's "teaching machine", evolving in the '70s to "response-and-branch" CBT, progressing into the '80s with Apple's "poke-and-see" hypercard and ultimately, "answer-vision", the hopes behind interactive video. All of these are examples of closed systems in which the content is pre-defined, responses are anticipated, and action is controlled by the designer alone. Interactive video pioneer, Andy Lippmann, lamented the inherent weakness of such closed systems. None seemed to satisfy his definition of interactivity, the mutual, autonomous, and simultaneous activity of both participants working toward a common goal. Lippman suggested five criteria which are necessary to satisfy this definition:

— interruptability, the ability of either participant to interrupt the other at any point.

— graceful degradation, the ability to set aside the unanswerable questions in a way that does not halt the conversation.

— limited look-ahead, the quality that makes it impossible to predict the ultimate outcome of a conversation by either party.

— no default, a quality which allows the shape of a conversation to develop naturally, organically, without a preplanned path.

— the impression of an infinite database, the quality of limitless choices and realistic responses to any possible input.

Lippman's criteria are fundamentally unreachable under the constraints of a closed technology. But the open architecture of the Internet transfers interactivity from an affordance of designer control to that of user control. From flat textual domains to full motion video, the Internet transforms the mechanistic character of modern media into a postmodern phenomenon, shifting agency from author to user. The designer has lost control, but the medium has gained credibility. We no longer have to contrive interactive "lessons" and exercises. The real world is waiting on the other side of the terminal. When we speak of affordances in the study of media, we are cautioned as designers to resist the assumption that a given medium affords a specific set of learning outcomes. In reality, learning is distributed between the medium, the learner and the context. There is nothing inherent in the Internet that guarantees learning. But in a specific context involving learning activities, such as research, collaboration, self expression, and reflection, the Internet offers multiple affordances, so numerous that it may be a mistake for us to treat it as a medium. It is really an infrastructure which brings together media, tools, people, places and information, expanding the range of human capabilities. If we treat the Internet as an infrastructure, then we can draw comparisons between the Internet and other infrastructures which society has come to rely upon for learning and education. These include:

— library
— publishing house
— school
— community
— city

We suggest that the Internet offers multiple affordances, not unlike other infrastructures for learning. And we suggest that the Internet overcomes significant factors which have historically constrained the others. A comparative analysis may illustrate our point.

Library

The library is an infrastructure containing multiple technologies working together to deliver specific information in response to an inquiry. The patron consults a data base (card catalog or electrónic index) to find a range of books which may contain the desired information. The patron selects the most appropriate listings from among those suggested, then proceeds to the locations in the library directed by each selection. For each book that is located, the patron consults its index and table of contents, then leafs though the pages to confirm whether the book holds pertinent information. If so, the information is eventually extracted and the task is complete. Research on the Internet involves a similar process. The user consults a database called a search engine.

A simple or structured query will yield a set of hits or listings, not unlike the selections from a library catalog. The user selects the most appropriate hits, retrieving each document electronically. Within seconds each target document is retrieved. A hypertext index or table of contents will allow the user to dip into the text wherever her interest leads. For plain text documents, the user can invoke a keyword search utility on her browser locating specific paragraphs of interest. Pertinent information is extracted and the task is complete. Like a library, the internet affords great potential for research.

The processes of information searching are similar, if not identical. The results are not so similar. At the present time, a good research library is likely to yield a higher quality result than the Internet. But the Internet is likely to yield more up-to-date information than a library. A comparison of constraints will reveal some important differences:

Schedule: A library is constrained by limited hours of operation. Serious researchers are painfully familiar with the signification of flickering lights toward the end of the library's service day. But the Internet is not constrained by schedule. It is as available as a personal computer and a modem.

Location: A library has a fixed location. Most communities have at least one library but rural communities are especially constrained. The Internet is not constrained by proximity. It is accessible anywhere that electronic communication is possible. Typically the electronic patron accesses Internet resource from home or from the work place.

Holdings: A library's holdings are constrained by past acquisitions and current budgets. Most libraries are able to overcome this constraint by interlibrary loans. The Internet is one huge virtual library whose holdings are growing daily. At the present time, resources on the Internet are fundamentally constrained by copyright.

Most books in print are available in book stores or at the library, but they can not be obtained online. This is not a natural constraint of the technology, but the result of lagging proprietary laws associated with prior technologies. Another constraint, at least for the present, is laborpower: the effort required to migrate public domain literature to electronic substrates. This is a noble effort, motivating thousands of volunteer scribes, but at this moment the bulk of the world's literature remains somewhere on a dusty shelf.

Accessibility: A library book is accessible within minutes, hours, days or weeks, depending on the book's location and availability. Electronic texts are available instantly. Checked-out and overdue documents are unknown in the virtual library. Research sessions need not be interrupted for lack of immediate access. What's more, instantaneous retrieval enables hypertext (linking between texts) as a research affordance—something not feasible with conventional print media.

Timeliness of holdings: Libraries receive information once it is published. Published information is usually well written, edited and thoroughly reviewed for accuracy. For most quality books, this process takes several months. New material finds its way to the Internet immediately. Many articles are accessible on the net months before they become published in print form. Authors often post early drafts of their work for purposes of feedback and peer review. The immediate overriding constraint of the Internet is the fact that few users have learned how to manipulate Internet tools with the same confidence that they can manipulate a library.

As the Internet evolves, we can observe the changes before our eyes. In the past two years, the number of text objects on the World Wide Web grew from several thousand to several million. The tools for extracting information showed their limitations as Internet holdings constantly increased. New tools have been laid down over the old, smarter, faster, yielding more astounding results. Tools are evolving in the direction of object-oriented simplicity. But users are hard-pressed to keep up with the changes. The implications for instruction and performance technology in this context are obvious.

Most of us learned how to use the Library when we were in school, and we learned by doing—doing research. In the process of solving research problems we had the scaffolding of librarians and the coaching of good teachers. We suggest that Internet skills deserve a similar treatment. The power of Internet resources remains latent to those without the skills to use them. But who are the librarians in this virtual library? Who will provide the scaffolding and coaching for the unskilled researcher? Who will undertake the task of conjoining people and knowledge. Who will classify knowledge and information? These tasks don't go away in the virtual environment, but the agency of librarianship shifts from the center to the periphery. The role of virtual librarian is distributed.

In the virtual library there is no central keeper of knowledge, only curators of particular views. The role of organizing and classifying knowledge is passed to each user. A user saves and organizes the information that is personally useful. As one's interests and knowledge become specialized, a niche emerges for a specific field of knowledge. The ones who use the information are the ones who will organize and classify that body of knowledge, primarily for personal use but also to serve the virtual community.

The intellectual labor invested in research is freely shared on the net as users make public the artifacts of their own knowledge construction: the bookmarks, lists and directories of information we compile for use in our own intellectual efforts. One person's artifact is another's affordance. We maintain a set of bookmarks related to Instructional Technology. While the work is a product of our own research for our own purposes, it can provide scaffolding for others with similar interests. By making public this entailment, we have the benefits of interaction with others who are drawn to the resource because of their own allied modes of inquiry. The ethic of sharing information, including classifications of this nature, is the emerging culture of the net. The motivation is no different than the traditional practice of publishing scholarly work.

Publishing

The publishing infrastructure has been the primary conduit for knowledge in the modern world. It requires capital and considerable labor to disseminate information in published form. Between the modern author and the reader is an infrastructure which includes editors, type setters, printers, binders, and a complex marketing and distribution organization.

For a publisher to print anything today, a business case must guarantee proper return on the investment. At a time when society's need for diverse information expands geometrically, the number of corporations which control the publishing infrastructure continues to decline. While freedom of the press is extended to all, its affordance is an exclusive privilege. The concept of free expression is changing as we pass from the modern to the postmodern. Having the right to free expression is something entirely different than having the affordance of expression. Just as technology challenged exclusive control of knowledge in the fifteenth century, exclusive control of information is challenged again today, this time by the Internet.

On the Internet, there is no central control: no editorial board to determine acceptability, no screening committee to determine relevance, no financial board to assess marketability. Each author is her own publisher. Each reader, his own editor. All that is required for publication on the World Wide Web is a personal computer, a modem, and a user account on an Internet server. Students and faculty enjoy such affordance at most major universities. Commercial providers offer public access at at costs comparable to telephone rates. Public schools are on the World Wide Web, publishing hypertext productions by teachers and students.

Today a third grader has the same affordance for expression as any other netizen, be they politicians, professors or published authors. What's more, her physical youth can be masked by her abilities of expression, making her a virtual equal among adult netizens. During the past decade, constructivist researchers have stressed the importance of anchoring instruction to genuine tasks in situated contexts. The Internet offers countless affordances toward that instructional goal. Consider a seventh grade class learning English grammar, spelling and rhetoric. Consider the World Wide Web as an affordance.

Imagine the possibility of our students providing a web page that is a genuine service to the Internet community, something the students care about, and something that is needed. Consider a likely niche, such as a weekly review of children's television, a computer help system for low-tech parents, a FAQ database on snow boarding, roller blading, etc.. Writing for an audience of peers around the world is likely to elicit motivations that go beyond teacher expectations. To the extent that students use the opportunity to present themselves before a world wide audience their writing will be influenced by motivations of ethos, style, and delivery: the elements of classical rhetoric. The constraining factors are likely to include the teacher's comfort level with the technology, and her willingness to yield control of the resource to her students, the level of her perception about the Internet as an affordance for learning goals (not necessarily for other institutional goals). The affordance of world wide public expression is something new for all of us. With the Internet, the perceived capability of self expression in a world-wide forum can be extended realistically to the common person. However, there is no expectation that each person will embrace it. Consider Socrates' reaction to literacy. Consider the skepticism of most Americans, saturated with the hype of technology and media. By definition, an affordance is the the potential for action. This implies that there is a will toward specific action. Implied in the affordance is the intentional desire for action and the recognition that the object can enable one's intentions.

For the reader, a fundamental constraint has to do with the accuracy, veracity and reliability of online information. This is not to say that accurate information can't be found on the net. The implication has more to do with the shifting role of the reader in assessing the accuracy, validity and applicability of materials which were heretofore left to editors, experts and peer professionals. An additional skill will be essential to our basic education—the skill of abductive logic.

The goal in abductive logic is not ultimate truth. It is the ability to advance one's inquiry. Abductive logic is the logic of signs: the ability to extract meaning from a given set of circumstances and then to adjust one's inquiry as new information unfolds. The skill of Sherlock Holmes is critical skill of the information age. There are Internet tools to assist in this process. They are called robots or agents. An agent is a software tool that is dispatched to accomplish a specific task. As information continues to abound on the Internet, we will need such tools to assist us in our searches. The standard tools are search engines which accept a set of keywords from a user and return a list of resources in rank order, listing first those which best match the search criteria. The problem is that searching on a single word can yield overwhelming and debilitating results. Stone suggests that the ideal model for an agent is the graduate student. Graduate students are trained to do research. They can assess the usefulness of new information within in the context of the present inquiry. A research assistant is attuned to a professor's work, and is able to gather the kind of information that fits a given research project. Can software agents be designed to fit that model? So-called intelligent search applications are available today. Instead of submitting a simple keyword, phrase or boolean expression, the user can submit a complex object: a bibliography, a list, an index, an article.

The intelligent agent discards incidental and common words from the text object, prioritizes the remaining words by the frequency of use. Multiple searches ensue, and results are evaluated against the model object. Tools of this nature produce quality results for minimal time investment, overcoming the debilitating constraints of too much information associated with simple searches. The fundamental characteristic of the Internet is that it cannot be controlled. While local legislation can influence pockets of control, the Internet is a world wide phenomenon, with no one in charge, (with everyone in charge). The Internet is not the McGuffy Reader. In more modern times educators could easily control what their students read and direct how those tender minds might be shaped. The educator's role was largely in the selection of good and proper literature, selecting resources which combined intellectual development with moral edification.

The learner's moral edification was directed externally by a teacher, by an editorial committee, or by a school board. Today the classics of literature, fine essays and poetry still abound. They are rapidly finding their way online. There will be a time in the next ten or fifteen years when every essay or poem that was ever published by McGuffy or any other reputable source will be available in digital format for readers who wish to partake of these edifying materials. But along side such uplifting literature will be objectionable material, countless resources of questionable value, some resources of objectionable content.

The supreme difficulty in the Information Age will be the ability to restrict a learner's education to a "sanctioned" body of literature. The discipline required of learners in the postmodern age goes beyond that of all previous generations. The role of education in the age of information will be the development of disciplined readers, skilled in the art of abductive logic.

Since we can no longer filter and select proper materials for our students, our highest calling as educators will be to support students in developing such discipline for themselves. Whitehead explained to an earlier generation of teachers that, "discipline is knowledge in the presence of freedom". Giving students the freedom to choose, then supporting them through the anguish of moral and logical choices, this is practice that builds discipline, skill, and moral fortitude. It will be the highest, most valued instructional model for the next few decades.

In contemplating what the future might hold for education it is sometimes useful to gaze into the past. We have attempted to show how formal knowledge broke free from cloistered protection to broad dissemination in the age of Guttenberg. Knowledge in the modern period followed logocentric patterns with one-to-many relationships. The postmodern period promises yet greater dissemination marked by a many-to-many relationships. The developments brought about by technology allow for new possibilities.

We are seeing trends in education toward distributed, collaborative models of learning. Agency is shifting from center to periphery, from teacher to learner, from author to reader, from librarian to researcher, from curriculum to context. The affordances of public expression have exploded, allowing any school child to represent herself before a world-wide community of learners.

The affordances of information retrieval have advanced to the point where a simple query can yield a flood of information. This is where the modern and postmodern minds collide. To the modern mind, there is too much information. The world is exploding with ideas and perspectives that cannot possibly be consumed. We must control what people read so that truth might prevail over misinformation, so that quality might prevail over mediocrity, so that correct ideas might prevail over anarchy. But to the postmodern mind, attempts to control information are futile and naive. What control exists in the postmodern world will emerge—not from the center, but from the periphery. The genie is out of the bottle. There is no chance of forcing him back. Modern educators have learned how to utilize constraints of the environment as a means of scaffolding in the instructional process. Constraints can limit a field of information, making it more manageable for learners. Constraints of grammar and syntax are necessary for language acquisition.

General social behavior is learned from constraints involving etiquette and protocol. We have shown that the Internet overcomes many of the constraints imposed by traditional educational infrastructures. But the freedoms that suddenly emerge are frightening. The modern educator might be tempted to impose artificial constraints on the medium in order to control and manage the educational environment. Software is available at this moment which allows a teacher or parent to filter information and restrict access to objectionable sources on the net. We acknowledge that such artificially imposed constraints may be necessary in the short run to mitigate controversial dilemmas and situations that challenge traditional thinking. But we are persuaded that the real challenge for education is to discover the natural constraints associated with a highly connected and deeply fragmented world.

A set of rules or policy guidebook for the postmodern will not be found. But out of distributed knowledge, we are seeing the emergence of a new ethic with an entailing structure of distributed control. The challenge for the postmodern educator is to discover the capabilities and natural constraints associated with distributed pedagogy for scaffolding learners in the age of information.

4

Interactive Online Learning

Many education and training institutions are looking at using the Internet for distance learning with renewed interest since the advent of graphical interfaces. Browsers, like Mosaic and Netscape, and the Web are making possible, the application of on-line multimedia technology in the distance learning environment. Distance educators are interested in this technology because of the potential improvements for interaction. This chapter reviews the interaction typically found in traditional (off-line) computer assisted instruction (CAIs) for possible implementation in HTML-based on-line tutorials.

The types of interaction, it is suggested that interaction typically found in traditional CAIs may fulfill only part of the interaction needed in effective distance learning programs that use on-line tutorials. Design recommendations are offered for HTML-based CAIs that may help incorporate a total interactive support package for distance learners. We begin here to address these issues; research will be needed to identify and develop sound implementation strategies in CMC delivered courseware.

Interaction & Distance Learning

Students in distance education are learners who have chosen this mode of study usually because of the flexibility it offers; students are not bound by time and location. This is evident considering that most distance learners are not isolated geographically from an institute of higher learning and could have chosen a program in traditional education instead. But interaction is often sacrificed for this gain in flexibility as a consequence of the barrier of distance between student, peers, and instructor.

This interaction has individual and social dimensions where individual interaction is interaction between the individual and the learning material and social interaction is interaction between two or more people concerning the learning material. Both forms of interaction are necessary for learning and should be ensured through the technology of the media and the design of the distance learning presentation. In 1993, the School of Computer Information and Science at Nova Southeastern University organized a multimedia research group to examine system and network issues and courseware development issues associated with the new technology on the Web.

Within the Courseware Development Team, a committee of the research group, members are looking at multimedia uses in traditional education for applicability to the computer media communications (CMC) distance learning environment (DLE). An initial review of how on-line tutorials were implemented at NSU revealed that most uses followed a hierarchical menu level approach with some interaction between student and tutorial and very little interaction between student and teacher (other than through outside communications) despite the potentiality of the hypertext environment through the Hypertext Transfer Protocol (HTTP) and associated HTML. Consequently, the team is investigating on-line CAI designs to improve individual and social interaction. Traditional CAI learner control strategies are being looked at for improving individual interaction and Common Gateway Interface (CGI) program support for social interaction.

Interaction Through Learner Control

Learner control is a characteristic of CAI where students are allowed to make decisions on the content and context of the CAI presentation, as opposed to program control where the learner has no opportunity for this type of interaction. This is not to say that program control CAI does not allow individual interaction. It is well understood that an individual can mentally interact with the knowledge domain of such programs, just like one interacts with a good novel, but cognitive learning theories suggest an interaction with the environment that shapes schemata and learner control is used to help facilitate this type of interaction.

The interaction implementation strategies in traditional CAI have primarily included content strategies where interaction is achieved through learner control techniques such as content control, sequence control, pace control, display (strategy) control, and feedback control. Context strategies are also used to give the learner control over the background setting and text density. Content control allows the learner to control the selection of the content he or she wishes to learn.

The CAI has a set of topics from which the student can select. Sequence control, like content control, allows the selection of subjects, but in this case, all the subjects or topics have learning objectives related to the overall course goal and the learners' control is over the sequence of the topics to be learned. Pace control is typically considered one of the strongest advantages of CAI. It is a form of individualized instruction which allows the learner to take as much time as necessary to learn the lesson concepts.

Usually, this type of control involves some kind of student tracking system so users can take up where they left off from the last CAI session. It also includes features that allow the student to control movement from one screen to another. Display control allows the learner to choose one of several displays which cover the same subject matter or concept. A rule, an example, and simulation, all covering the same material, can be provided to allow the learner to select which options they personally need in order to grasp the lesson concepts. Feedback control allows the learner to either defer to computer controlled feedback or select options on the feedback mechanism. Context control includes learner control over the background of the material and text density.

Principles and concepts can be presented in different environments which serve as the backdrop to the lessons and also provide a form of situated learning. Mathematical concepts, for example, can be presented as business, or scientific problems and the user is free to choose the situation. Text density refers to the density of the material presented—bullet statements as opposed to explanatory paragraphs, etc.

Implementation Strategies of Learner Control

The learner control classifications by examining the strategy of the controlling implementation as opposed to the control mechanisms. They found that whatever type of control mechanism used, the implementation strategy generally fell into two categories.

— An approach where the entire lesson is presented to the student and the student has positive control to eliminate unwanted material.

— An approach where only basic and fundamental principles are presented to the student and the student has positive control to add to the material. They called these two approaches as "FullMinus" and "LeanPlus" respectively.

In a study using these two approaches and variations with incentive, the FullMinus group performed only marginally better than the LeanPlus group; however, learner behaviour showed that the FullMinus group was able to cover more material in the same amount of time and this group had a more favourable attitudinal response than the LeanPlus group so there would seem to be a case for a FullMinus approach in the learner control strategy.

Learner control can be applied through a Web structure although some content methods may be more difficult than others. The HTTP protocol allows branching of documents and can be used for both content control and sequence control. Pace control is already inherent in distance education and providing a student tracking system within the CAI would require additional programming or CGI support. Feedback control is limited by the basic HTML standard but can be improved greatly with the addition of CGIs. Display control and context methods of control appear well within the educator's ability to implement using HTML. Learner control strategies like FullMinus and LeanPlus also seem possible. Another challenge using HTML in CAI design actually results from the strength of the Web.

The Web was originally designed to facilitate the growth of non-linear knowledge bases throughout the Internet. Users are free to enter works at different locations (documents) and they can establish these entries within their own home pages. A CAI, even one with extensive branching, tends to be a single work that expects students to begin at the same location and end at some defined criteria level. The paths between the two may be different for each student but the beginning is usually the same.

Students' power to enter the works at any location may not meet the CAI designer's intent so the design of each document within the work must be able to stand alone so that confusion is not caused by references to previous topics not visibly seen. This capability to enter the work at any document location, on the other hand, might be a method of learner control unique to the distance learning environment, yet to be explored.

When one examines past studies on learner control in CAI in traditional settings, a general impression is formed that interaction, discussed in these studies between a student and CAI, is a representation of interaction (social) between the student and teacher/ designer who authored the CAI program. It probably goes without disagreement, this implied social interaction may actually occur by other means; communications with peers or SME. The central problem in the distance learning environment is that the effectiveness of the programmed interaction through learner control strategies may not be sufficient, in itself, to improve social interaction in the absence of other communications.

There has been unanimous agreement among distance education theorists that two-way communications is an essential element in distance education. By looking at the learning situation, it helps to visualize where social interaction strategies are needed to improve student-teacher interaction in HTML-based CAIs.

Improving Social Interaction

The need for student-to-SME knowledge base interaction. In this scenario, the student is taking the CAI and is confronted with an issue of special interest the student wishes to explore further by browsing related literature immediately. If the instructor has been maintaining a home page with an index into the knowledge domain, HTML links could be strategically placed into the tutorial to allow the student to deviate from the planned course of instruction to investigate related material. This is a unique form of learner control that can be implemented on the Web which goes beyond traditional CAI uses of branching. With Web tools, totally unplanned and unprogrammed excursions are made available to the student. The student is literally interacting with the instructor's knowledge and the instructor's Internet links to the knowledge base of the subject matter. Now consider the need for student-to-SME direct communications. In this scenario, the student is taking the CAI and is confronted with material that is confusing, or the student wants to add information, or take issue with the presentation.

The student wishes to communicate with the instructor on the subject. In traditional CAI, the student can normally have face-to-face human interaction with the CAI subject expert at the next scheduled class session but in distance education, this is not always possible. The distance learner must make a mental note and then contacts the instructor by telephone, e-mail, or written correspondence and this delay may cause the spirit of the message to be diluted.

With HTML/CGI forms technology, it would be possible to add hypernotes write capability to the on-line CAI that would allow email communications with the instructor while taking the CAI. Finally, consider the need for instructor-to-student communications. Just as any teacher wishes to monitor student progression in the class room in order to help redirect when necessary, in this scenario, the instructor wishes to monitor the progress of students as they interact with the CAI.

HTML/CGI might provide the capability to input student performance measures and CAI file access times into a data file which can be reviewed periodically by the instructor, and used to gauge student progression through the CAI, thus identifying student problems early on. The instructor would be able to generate follow-up messages to students.

HTML CAI design characteristics

The following considerations are offered: It is possible to have no learner control by establishing the work (presentation) as a single document (file). The entire work would look much like an electronic version of a printed paper and would have no links to any other documents. Very basic learner control could be added to the document with a table of contents that links to internal document anchors.

The advantage of this traditional approach to on-line Web documentation are the file can be easily printed or downloaded by students and less links may offer less access time; an economical concern. Improving interaction will lessen these advantages and should be cautiously considered in light of different learning styles but used where appropriate. Once the work is divided into linked documents, learner control over content and sequence greatly improves, but will be unrestricted in that the user can establish their own home pages and links to augmented sources.

The author should exploit this capability in the learner control strategy instead of considering it a liability, and should realize that the work may evolve into a complex web of information (improving social interaction in the cyber community) by the learner's actions as additional links are established to other sources. Such a learning environment may likely be reserved for advanced learning situations.

Since a FullMinus learner control strategy is apparently more effective than a LeanPlus strategy in traditional uses of tutorials, an on-line tutorial that introduces new concepts should contain as much required information as possible and students can use the learner control capabilities of item two to filter unwanted information.

On the other hand, a LeanPlus strategy might prove more useful than the FullMinus strategy in a tutorial that is designed to reinforce concepts previously learned. The tutorial could list other Web source documents or search engines that the student could linked to if desired. Text density is another area of great promise for on-line tutorials. Tutorial authors can develop two or more versions of each document within the work that would allow the learner the choice between abbreviated or expository information.

Despite the unrestricted content and sequence control inherent in an HTML work, authors should establish navigation features within each document that help users to move within the design originally envisioned by the author. The user, of course, is free not to use the navigation features, but for beginners, these features might be an indispensable help aid. An orientation strategy should be used to add visibility to the structure of the entire work. Graphical presentations have been shown to be more effective at this than text based.

A map of the presentation should be included and navigation methods to the map should be available within each document. The graphical map, however, must use HTML alternative methods since some students may only have text based browsers or have elected to turn off the graphical capabilities of advanced browsers in order to improve performance in data transfer.

The protocol for HTML forms allows data input by the user into a database file or electronic mail. Link objects could be added to the tutorial that students could activate when they need to contact the instructor. The instructor could review comments daily and respond to students as necessary. Using HTML supported by CGI, implement tracking methods to gauge student performance through CAIs. Design them so that student problems can be easily identified and instructors can give feedback to students as early as possible.

The use of learner control strategies in traditional CAI has been study extensively and is still on-going as technologies change the learning environment. We can use this research to help design learner control strategies for on-line tutorials. Additional research in learner control for on-line applications, however, will be needed to understand individual interaction in the on-line environment, with all its own technological challenges and constraints. Also needed are studies in the design of on-line CAI to see if there is any impact on social dimension of interaction.

The increased use of educational technology is only a minor aspect of the redesign of courses for flexible delivery, but the technology can be a source of considerable stress both for staff and for students. As more teachers make use of the Web for delivery of courses and for interaction with students, the careful choice of software tools can reduce this stress by providing interfaces that are easy to drive, thus reducing the cognitive overhead for staff and for students. The still-developing WEST educational management system provides a simple consistent interface to many of the communication and interaction tasks teachers need to carry out in constructing and managing courses that make use of the Web.

Changing the Location of Learning

Over the next few years many of us will benefit from and also be burdened by the need for learning to extend beyond the physical location of the University and also beyond the early years of life. The most predictable outcome of this change is that our teaching will increasingly make use of the Internet, the vast and continually growing web of networked computers that can be accessed by students both from their homes and from the University. We will have to learn many new skills to maintain our competency as educators. Most University staff enjoy learning, but the methods of learning they mastered may not be as comfortably available to our students in our joint future.

As our society moves from universal secondary education to universal tertiary education we will increasingly be subject to pressures designed to influence us to make the University experience more accessible, allowing busy people to fit it in to their working day when they see fit. We will lessen the disruption to students' lives by reducing the need for them to travel to the central University site in order to engage with the University experience. We will do this in part by providing learning interactions through a variety of electronic communications. Universities who fail to make such a concession to their students' needs will undoubtedly lose students to one of the developing Virtual Universities.

Flexible Learning and Teaching

Introducing flexible teaching involves a lot more than merely converting lecture notes into Web pages. On the visual level the differing characteristics of the media require quite different formatting of textual material. On the organisational level, breaking the lock-step of classroom sessions and mass concurrent teaching will require much greater flexibility on the part of the bureaucracy, as exemplified in the negative by the current insistence of many institutions on students' personal attendance for re-enrolment. Considerable anguish may be caused for lecturers who will need to rewrite much of their teaching material if they are to avoid high dropout rates and take advantage of the increased opportunities for their students to experience the realia of a subject.

The loss of face-to-face behavioural, gestural and tonal cues may give rise to many misunderstandings and will require particular attention in our educational designs. Many teachers have to imitate existing familiar teaching situations and strategies when delivering instruction via new technologies, and the problems this approach causes in the successful adoption of the new technologies. Besides raising the need for staff development in the use of new teaching media, they point out that two of the 'missing' components in conventional distance education are student/instructor interaction and class collaboration. Retaining the immediacy of these learning interactions will not be accidental. New communication technologies now allow us provide much more of these than in conventional distance education, but the design task is not trivial even for single-user interactive media.

Learning from a well-made Open Learning package may be like having a good human coach or tutor, but the skills involved in preparing that package are quite different from those required to deliver a useful lecture.

Beyond these issues, however, many operational difficulties arise in our use of such educational communication technologies, as we have experienced in the adoption of earlier technologies in face-to-face teaching.

The use of video-projection from a computer to replace the use of static overheads does not dispose of the need to prepare a certain amount of static overhead material as a backstop in case the video-projection system fails. For differing reasons, this doubled preparation will be repeated as we introduce more flexible methods into our teaching. Both the face-to-face or audio-taped lecture and the Web page need to be prepared if we are to provide increased flexibility rather than merely a substitution of delivery media. While in an ideal University there would be sufficient support staff to relieve the lecturer of the technological aspects of this task, experience suggests that the present dearth of such support staff will continue, a lack both in absolute numbers and specifically of those who are sensitive to and have some allegiance to the needs of teaching as opposed to the needs of machines.

Teaching staff will have to bear at least part of the preparation burden, just as many now prepare their own teaching aids such as overheads. The temptation for many will be the direct conversion of existing material for electronic presentation. This will create a market for conversion software, able to ease the task for relatively non-technical teaching staff, as programs such as Powerpoint have done over the last few years. In the short term many electronic lectures will be created, driven by the pressures of time and lack of support and justified as being at least partial steps along the way to providing more flexible learning conditions.

Situated Learning

Learning activities that lack social interaction usually fail to evoke emotional involvement from learners and thus deny the learners engagement with the culture of the "community of practice". Most classroom learning activities involve knowledge which is abstract and out of context, is unsituated. Problem-based learning approaches tend to reduce these effects and well-made multimedia interactives can restore some context to the learning, but teaching that interposes current communication technology between the learner and the teacher risks engaging the student with the wrong "community of practice". The technologically-aware lecturer needs to be sensitive to the danger of having students apprenticed to technology rather than their chosen discipline.

Reduction of Personal Contact

In contrast to the pressure towards "remote-control" teaching will be our desire to maintain the personal contacts that we see as necessary and valuable in understanding and guiding our students. Mass teaching has reduced this contact and the use of educational technology can sometimes lead to further depersonalisation.

Teachers seek to ameliorate this depersonalisation by, for example, trying to make the mass lecture a two-way communication: standing at the front of the theatre while showing slides: setting aside times when they are available for personal discussions in their office. The increased use of technology dictated by our move to greater flexibility needs to be leavened where possible by increased interactions between student, teacher and learning community. We should try to avoid techniques and technologies which isolate learners from one another, seeking rather to identify tools which, because of their ease of use, are more likely to used both by students and staff.

Internet Communication

In the broad educational context, the use of Internet software is likely to increase as a channel for communication between learner and teacher. A partial list of desired communications includes:

1 free-form text messages between lecturer and individual students and vice-versa email software, Eudora

2 messages from lecturer to entire class mailing list software

3 delivery of learning materials and assignments to student when, where and as they need them Telnet, Fetch or Gopher session, or a Web page with links to download files to the student's own machine

4 response by student to short structured questions to allow lecturers and students to assess learning achieved forms-based Web pages backed with CGI scripting to extract results

5 text-based commentary between students about the learning resources IRC Chat session or computer conference

6 transfer of image files between students for discussion, together with manipulation of such

images visible to many students concurrently whiteboard facility included in many forms of desktop video conferencing

7 submission of assignments by students electronically, together with return of assignments to students by the lecturer email with attached documents

8 synchronous audio communication between a student or students and the lecturer audio-conference equipment, party-line call or Internet Phone

9 asynchronous audio communication between relevant parties answering machine or audio download from a Web page

10 face-to-face visual communication between a student or students and the lecturer video-conference, desktop video-conference or CUSeeMe call

Current affordable network tools supporting remote learners allow email, file transfer, computer conferencing and Web browsing, but these various tools demand a serious learning effort from their users, not only from the students as learners but also from their lecturers as administrators. This extra learning effort adds an additional barrier between learner and teacher, between learner and learning. The use of a computer in the message-passing stream can be considered an impediment to learning for many students. In addition, the lead-time and response-time in student-teacher interactions are lengthened. With paper and chalkboard, these times are quite small. Involving a bureaucracy in assignment reception and registration can add weeks to the interaction process.

Using electronic communications that require reprocessing and involve an educational technician may also slow the process enormously unless the lecturer takes action to minimise delays, preferably by retaining as much control as possible. Just as the growth of desktop publishing has benefited semiprofessional authors by passing control over the appearance of a work from the printer back to the author and reducing the overall production time, Web publishing and course management tools need to be put into the hands of teachers to retain as much immediacy as possible in student-teacher interactions.

Integration

Over time easier methods of achieving these varieties of educational interactions will be developed. The GUI Web browser integrates image and context, enhancing understanding and usability beyond the Gopher browser that gave access to similar material. Just as a Web browser allows file transfer, gopher access and email with little cognitive overhead required of the "reader", so the interface to the varieties of communication required in delivering a course and managing student interactions must be simplified. It will ease this exchange by reducing the need for the student to master the use of a variety of programs. These new integrated tools will also make it easier for teaching staff to manage the flow of material to and from their students. By making the process easier, the new tools leave more mental energy available for creativity and communication. Consequently both creation and communication are more likely to occur.

A variety of such learning management tools are being introduced as many Universities around the world reinvent their particular wheel. Products such as PacerForum and Lotus Notes, are restricted to use on a local area network or to organisations large enough to afford dedicated technical support for the groupwork system. Newer teaching and communication tools are frequently based on the use of the Web as this offers a pleasant and consistent graphical user interface and avoids many of the problems arising from the wide variety of computers that our students use.

Learning Management by the Lecturer

Where learning material is essentially static and designed to be read and copied by students, it can be stored on a university's Web server computer and maintained by emailing updates to Computing Centre staff directly or by file transfer using tools such as Fetch. If, however, you want to retain the more personal elements of teaching that many staff find rewarding, you may be interested in communicating on an individual level with your off-campus students, receiving and managing student responses, assignments and enquiries online, promoting class-wide discussion of a topic or even adjusting course material for individual student differences. WEST is a system developed at University College Dublin which makes it easier to manage the creation and delivery of learning materials over the Web. The ease with which this system can be set up and maintained puts it well within the technical ability of the majority of university computer users.

Once the server is running, all lecturer tasks can in fact be carried out from any computer on the network. If the current interest in using the Web to increase the flexibility of course offerings is maintained, personal Web servers backed by management systems like WEST could proliferate on lecturers' desktops, just as presentation software has become a standard part of the lecturer's toolk it. Just as HTML and its associated tools offer "multimedia for the rest of us", desktop educational support tools may add real value to the "ubiquitous servers" in educational institutions.

The system presents a simple consistent interface making heavy use of buttons and forms, as shown in the Figures below, thus avoiding the need for staff and students to master a variety of different interfaces to achieve the mix of messaging most appropriate to flexible learning. The WEST system provides facilities for individual registration and controlled access by students who are part of a class studying some course; it allows the allocation of learning materials as Web pages to students or to the whole class; it provides one-to-one messaging between student and tutor and between students. It also allows one-to-many messaging similar to a bulletin board or news group.

Students can send messages to their tutor and submit assignments. They can also send messages to specific students or to the entire class through the open-to-everyone discussion list, where they can read what other students have written about a course discussion topic. The simple interface of the discussion list is easy to understand and use but lacks the thread feature of Internet News.

Tutors can receive messages and assignments from students, reply, mark and return assignments or have them automatically marked and returned. They can make announcements to the whole class or address individual students. Any of the variety of messages can include HTML code and thus include hypertext references to other resources on the Internet. The use by students of simple Web server software will allow multimedia messaging between all participants. Administration of the system, including the addition, alteration or removal of content, classes and students. A lecturer can use dial in access to receive, send, create or modify materials using a Mac, Windows or Unix computer at home.

HTML must be written or pasted into the form as shown below. This is a far cry from the ease of such Web-page authoring tools as Adobe PageMill, but the body section of pages created in a Web editor can be copied and pasted into WEST. The instructional material can include links to any other page on the Web, as well as any of the usual variety of embedded Web-delivered multimedia, such as photographs and diagrams, Quicktime movies, Director animations and RealAudio streaming sound.

The WEST system currently runs as an Asynchronous CGI application only on Macintosh servers running MacHTTP or WebStar. The Webstar server software costs about A$250 and a single-server educational-use WEST licence for 10 simultaneous users (no limit to total users) costs about A$300. Versions of the WEST software for Unix and Windows NT are in beta now. The WEST system is used in the USA, Canada and Ireland for courses varying from a resource of information and research on Chemistry to delivery and management of course material for a multi-disciplinary Open Learning course on the Famine in Ireland.

WEST does not keep track of student accesses, nor of how far a student has progressed. These are important features for staff administering courses for remote students, whose flagging motivation may require restorative action unnecessary for on-campus students. Many teachers will need to learn new ways of teaching as flexible teaching and learning become an expected part of our course design and delivery. The design of material for learning at a distance is not a trivial task, but it will be made easier if the hurdles of Educational Technology can be lowered. Hopefully tools such as WEST will be improved without losing their ease of use and will allow teachers to incorporate a variety of message streams into their course material, to build in interactions that involve their students. If teachers can manage learning processes on the Internet without becoming amateur programmers, they will be able to give more attention to encouraging student-teacher and student-student interactions that are appropriate to the new media and the new learning environment.

5

Information Technology in Virtual Education

The "management of knowledge" in education, and, specifically, in efforts at educational reform. Schools and districts in the United States face mounting pressure to demonstrate the measurable effects of their practices to legislators, parents, the business world, and the public at large. This fact by itself adds to the information management burden placed on the educational system. However, other changes, such as the rise in student mobility and ethnic diversity, have increased the complexity of already complex school data systems. This complexity is rooted in the operational requirements of implementing and assessing instructional interventions and the interactions between racial, ethnic, and socioeconomic characteristics on student learning. The permutations of analytically distinct groups increase knowledge management burdens at an alarming rate. As growing diversity has been matched by increasing disparities in educational outcomes between a number of groups—poor and affluent, white and minority, urban and suburban—a patchwork of uncoordinated programs have been introduced at all education levels by a variety of government entities. This ad hoc form of policymaking often results in programs that at best do not reinforce one another and at worst actively work to undermine each other.

A more promising response, which has developed over the past decade, has been what is referred to as systemic or standards-based reform. Systemic reform, according to US Deputy Secretary of Education is typically based on state-level reforms that implement more rigorous content and performance standards across grades and disciplines. Systemic reform requires that curricular material and assessments be aligned with these standards. Preservice teacher education and teacher professional development must also support these goals. Finally, funding, technology, physical plant, and human resources must all be allocated in such a way that each group has equal access to the things it needs in order to succeed. To improve student achievement and to close the equity gap are the ultimate goals of systemic reform efforts, but supporters of systemic reform believe these goals can only be achieved by improving all aspects of the educational system. Major systemic reform initiatives at the national level seek to strengthen teacher education, reinvigorate the development of high-strength curriculum, and promulgate disciplinary standards. Some of these programs operate under the auspices of the US Department of Education and the National Science Foundation.

The majority of reforms are state-level initiatives to improve the performance of students in specific subject areas or grade ranges such as elementary reading or middle school mathematics. Individual districts also engage in reform initiatives that seek to motivate particular schools or groups of students to meet individual standard components. Finally, individual schools and classroom teachers work to develop lesson plans to teach concepts based on grade-level standards. These trends and the consequent emergence of more data-rich environments raise the need for new technologies and new management techniques for coping with complexity. Three technical issues in particular appear to be especially crucial.

— The problem of accurately identifying policy targets. Identifying the target group and the desired outcomes for a particular reform is necessary if one is to describe, analyze, and locate reform efforts within educational systems. Existing organizational identifiers such as school, classroom, or demographic data are often inadequate to isolate for study or evaluation students or teachers who participated in particular programs or received distinct treatments. The ability to accurately compare analytically distinct groups is vital if one is to assess the impact of systemic reform.

— Managing data. It is evident that successful systemic reform will depend on access to and effective use of large amounts of data. This means that the quantity, timeliness, and level of detail of the data needed from decision-support systems will only increase. Proponents of systemic reform point to the importance of a process model and evaluation framework for assessing programs. The process of systemic reform must include actors from all levels and it must include an awareness of resources and barriers confronting actors across educational roles. The focus on process also points to the importance of quality indicators. Quality measures might include a detailed analysis of curriculum goals and well-understood, publicly available education standards. High quality instruction demonstrates an alignment between standards, curriculum, and assessment. The difficulty of measuring differential interventions is compounded by the need to gauge the quality and thoroughness of new, robust curricula and to obtain more detailed analyses of student progress.

— Metrics, i.e., multiple-choice versus authentic-performance tasks. Demands for more authentic assessments have led to calls for new metrics of student performance relative to standards, as well as an emphasis on measuring a particular student's attainment of individual proficiencies. The new standards-based approaches have led to the creation of new sorts of testing that go beyond the typical fill in the bubble standardized assessments.

The introduction of multifaceted testing regimes (including traditional standardized tests, as well as performance and portfolio-based assessments) both increases the complexity of the individual instruments and creates new requirements for the underlying data systems that must both record and provide an analytical environment for the data. The increasing sophistication of assessment practices calls for a parallel development in the arena of information-management strategies. The technical aspects of fundamental research questions—What to study? How to aggregate the data? And what are the appropriate measures? As our understanding of the educational process deepens, our technical capacity to collect, manage, and analyze data must keep pace. The growing body of literature on knowledge management (based primarily on research coming out of United States and European business schools) to the specific case of systemic reform in US education. Knowledge management (KM) strategies can serve as valuable tools for decision makers at all levels of the educational system. The distinctive features of knowledge management, identifying the characteristics of successful KM efforts and exploring the usefulness of KM for making important educational decisions. With a discussion of the role of information technology (as a component of a KM system) in the implementation of high-stakes accountability for 8th grade students in one particular urban district.

Before considering the characteristics of knowledge management, it is important to note the differences between data, information, and knowledge. Which presents the argument that knowledge is a product that is built from data and information, provides the following definitions:

> It is perhaps easiest to understand knowledge in terms of what it is not. It is not data and it is not information. Data are objective facts, presented without any judgment or context. Data becomes information when it is categorised, analysed, summarized, and placed in context.
>
> Information therefore is data endowed with relevance and purpose. Information develops into knowledge when it is used to make comparisons, assess consequences, establish connections, and engage in a dialogue. Knowledge can, therefore, be seen as information that comes laden with experience, judgment, intuition, and values.

There is a clear progression along the path in which value is added to data, as context is combined with it to create information. A further transformation occurs when human experience is added to information to make value judgments about, and comparisons of, different information. The progression from data to knowledge can be seen both as a temporal process in which data, imported into a system's architecture, aggregates individual facts into summaries and averages that are then presented in an appropriate context. In an educational setting, this might be a report of student test performance by grade, ethnicity, race, and gender.

The addition of deeper contextual information about local school leadership, particular organizational characteristics, or other less quantifiable factors can be combined with mechanistically generated test-score results to describe variance in outcomes that could not be extracted from the more traditional reports. It is this application of personal knowledge and of well-designed models that differentiates information systems from knowledge systems.

KM is a follow-up to information management. The bulk of the literature on good information system design focuses on the technologies and processes used to acquire and manage data. When describing the breadth of approaches to effective knowledge use, a number of authors describe a range of system functions from data management to knowledge creation and application. Information management lies somewhere between the two poles of data management and knowledge management. Another way to think about KM is that it is the use or application of information. In districts, the student data system provides the core of such a system. However, this focus on information systems and tools for aggregation and on KM as the application of information should not imply some type of computer-based system that is somehow imbued with deep contextual knowledge of the organization. This is not just a question of the technologies employed. An important role is played by institutional culture. For example, a district with a collaborative model of interaction between schools will typically display a far greater capacity to develop robust analyses of school-level processes and needs than a district lacking such a model.

The importance of organizational culture in enabling or blocking the use of knowledge. Cultures that support knowledge accumulation and application will be the most effective, efficient organizations. Organizational structures and processes provide a window into the value a knowledge management system will return to any implementer. A willingness to engage in problem-solving processes and share information with outsiders is an important resource for enabling knowledge management efforts. What is the goal of this organization's knowledge management strategy? Davenport and his colleagues conducted a study of 31 KM projects across 24 companies. The authors identified four broad types of objectives with different subtypes:

— Create knowledge repositories–

a) external knowledge (competitive intelligence, market data, surveys, etc.),

b) structured internal knowledge (reports, marketing materials, techniques and methods), and

c) informal internal knowledge (discussion databases of 'know how' or 'lessons learned').

In an educational setting, curriculum aids might be thought of as knowledge repositories. For example, the Milwaukee Public Schools Curriculum Design Assistant

(CDA) is both a source of documentation—standards, learning goals, etc.—and a repository for instructional plans based on this documentation. These lesson plans can be stored in the system and shared with others electronically to provide a knowledge base for a wider audience.

— Improve knowledge accessthrough

a) technical expert referral,

b) expert networks used for staffing based on individual competencies, and

Examples of this sort in public school education are probably rare, but the Community of Science online database is a data and communication resource that functions well in education research: it links researchers, research intuitions, and funders together. The purpose of the Community of Science online database is to reduce the barriers for those seeking funding for research, as well as to reduce the difficulty of funders in locating qualified researchers.

— Enhance the knowledge environment –

a) change organizational norms and values related to knowledge in order to encourage knowledge use and knowledge sharing,

b) customers may be asked to rate their provider's expertise.

This objective focuses on the creation of a technological environment that will contribute to the social transformation of an organization. Anderson Consulting used this sort of approach to radically shift norms of information sharing and use among its consulting staff. In the consulting business, there are traditionally strong norms about keeping personal expertise personal—it represents a large portion of individual competitive advantage. Anderson Consulting wanted to reverse this behavior and reward those who shared information with other consultants within the organization.

The company began to make participation in an online, e-mail-based, problem-solving environment mandatory. Eventually the bar was raised further and pay and promotion were linked to the number, quality, and immediacy of an individual's responses. This approach was draconian, but it was successful in building both a compelling repository of problem-solving information and shifting or overturning a strong norm against sharing information. This approach models an important tool for accumulating and diffusing successful educational practices. The call for methods of replicating successful programs and school initiatives that beat the odds could be addressed with a system that improves communication within educational systems.

— Manage knowledge as an asset–

a) attempt to measure the contribution of knowledge to bottom line success.

While this final KM objective sounds the most compelling, it is also the most difficult to operationalize. Even firms with excellent data-management practices and sophisticated conceptions of return on investment have difficulty assessing the return on intangibles. Learning Landscape is an example of one such effort in education. This system was an outgrowth of the Connecticut Academy's NSF-sponsored Statewide Systemic Initiative. The Connecticut Academy worked together with the consulting firm, KPMG, to develop a data warehouse environment based on the National Center for Education Statistics core data elements. The stated purpose of the chapter was to transform data into knowledge to improve student achievement and teacher quality. This chapter was abandoned after it became clear that the development costs would exceed what most districts would be able to afford.

A new firm has been established, EdExplore, which has the same KM goals but is much more limited in scope and has implementation costs in line with district resources. EdExplore remains focused on bringing cutting-edge approaches to data warehousing to the evaluation of student and teacher performance. These different goals are not mutually exclusive. Davenport states that most projects his team studied were focused on one of these goals, but many had features of the other goals interwoven into their projects. In addition, the first three objectives can be seen as constituting a feedback loop. Repositories must be built. Then, these repositories are only useful if users have efficient access to the knowledge contained in them. Finally, the use of knowledge in an organization will be enhanced by the creation of an environment that supports this use. This knowledge-friendly environment will, in turn, demand higher levels of sophistication in the knowledge repository, thus closing the loop.

The fourth goal—determining the return on investment in knowledge management—is closely related to efforts that attempt to determine the return on investment from spending on early research and development. Many analysts have struggled with this vexing issue, which remains only partly addressed. There are so many unquantifiable, human elements in a KM system that it may be very difficult to come up with metrics that are generalizable.

Knowledge Networks

There are several problems that must be faced by any educational system that attempts to create a knowledge management system. The first problem is to determine the appropriate level of analysis the system is designed to support. Another is that of differential access to computing power and the technical and analytical skills of the knowledge consumers within the system. In an educational setting, users representing students, classroom teachers, principals, and district administration should be involved in the design of a system destined to support important instructional and policy-level decision making. It is only by including users at all levels of the knowledge system that designers will have the input necessary to grapple with the problems identified above. The knowledge management systems provide very little insight into the exact analytical approaches one would use in any particular scenario, since so much depends on the organizational form, sector, or level of analysis.

The discussions in the literature focus instead on families of tools designed for pattern detection and predictive modeling. It is important to bring these together with the experience of those working in the specific domain to identify the important dimensions of knowledge in that field, since we have defined knowledge as the application of information in context. A crucial feature of educational systems is that they are made up of a number of nested systems or organizations. In analytical terms, this can also be described as levels or units of analysis. In education, these levels range from the federal level, through the state, district, school, classroom, and student levels.

The analytical needs differ from level to level as do the relevant time scales. For example, there are classroom needs for lesson planning and local testing. At the school level, free lunch, state-mandated testing, and other mandated programs are focal points of data-management issues. The requirements are as numerous as the funding sources at each level of the organization. Analytical needs differ, but are present at every level of the system. A robust knowledge management system must reflect the information and knowledge management needs of all levels. In particular, data must be gathered at a level of aggregation appropriate to the user with the most fine-grained analytical needs.

The most common focus of school information systems is on the school and district-level, produced by a central information technology department. In the case of school district-level knowledge management systems, one might attempt to implement several KM systems. One could argue that schools are groups of professionals with both process and content knowledge. One organizational model used to describe reform-based schools—communities of practice—would suggest that they would be more likely to focus on enhancing a knowledge environment. Operating under this model, schools would be less likely to accumulate knowledge for its own sake. They would focus, instead, on sharing knowledge among a group of professionals. This would be consistent with the view that schools are communities of learners.

A KM system that supports such behavior would be both a repository of successful practices and a system for conveying positive norms associated with sharing knowledge. The importance of the level of analysis comes to the forefront of any effort to describe and apply KM principles. For example, district-level functions might include analysis of the quality of the data in the system (this may be in formal terms of validity and/or reliability, as well as of alignment of the metrics in use and the learning or performance standards). District-level analysis might also focus on the curricula that are in use across the district and assess their relative effectiveness. These district-level functions call for nested hierarchies of approaches to systems design that support collection of the relevant data and aggregation of these data to the appropriate level of analysis. The identification of distinct levels in an organization with different KM needs is even more vital if one considers the increasing demands technology places on individual units in an organization.

The traditional neoclassical economics concept of a linear relationship among the different factors of production fails to adequately explain the returns of knowledge. One moves up within an organization, the number of elements that must be integrated in order to produce a good or service has probably not increased dramatically in recent years. However, the pace at which new technologies and needs are introduced and old technologies become obsolete has increased dramatically. This rapid pace of change in the factors of production places a premium on the ability of individuals within an organization to track change and respond to it. This ability is one of the key features of successful KM. Unfortunately, this is an area in which traditional information management systems.

Data warehouse systems are excellent tools for making complex selections of data from many different sources. However, there are no good inferential or predictive models in place within commercial school decision support systems for modeling school or student behavior in real time. This is not because there is not a rich understanding of student achievement. Rather, the cost and complexity of real-time KM systems represent a major obstacle to schools or districts taking advantage of this technology. Schools have lagged behind industry in replacing paper-based clerical and business functions (often referred to as back office functions) with technology-based systems. They often lack the physical infrastructure necessary for communication between numerous geographically dispersed buildings.

Access to Computing Power

The rise of ubiquitous computing, which places relatively inexpensive devices for information storage and manipulation on every desk, has made the conversion to technology-based systems possible. This trend is now finding its way into schools as they move away from using computers for rote learning to employ them as information tools. This is not simply a centralization-decentralization issue—i.e., the spread of technology from the district to the school and classroom. These resources can serve additional goals outside of instruction. A personal computer is both an information-gathering and an information-manipulation tool. The availability of computing at all levels of the educational system can be a focal point of change. There are certainly budget, security, and management implications in broadening access to sophisticated computing technologies. However, the need for information transcends district governance issues Moves toward greater local autonomy and responsibility—whether in response to school vouchers, charter initiatives, or other pressures—mean that there will be an increasing need for local analytical capacity.

The need for well-informed local decision-making at the classroom level is not unique to any particular organizational form, however, such as block scheduling, or multi-age classrooms. It exists in both flat and hierarchical organizations. The level at which decisions are made may differ across organization types, but there must still be robust data-collection and knowledge-dissemination mechanisms at all levels. This is particularly important given the different uses of individual data elements at different levels of aggregation and at different levels of the organization. Even at the school level, one can demonstrate the utility of comparing groups such as students who are bussed versus not bussed, or students participating in a specific after-school program versus students who do not. Traditional aggregations of data in such instances prove inadequate.

The problems outlined above suggest several possible avenues of system design that would lead to more appropriate data structures and produce more useful knowledge in an education knowledge management setting. The focus on student learning, and the persistent gaps in student achievement described above, should suggest to system designers that knowledge management systems should be student focused. What this means is that individual student data must comprise the basic building block of any knowledge management system in education. This includes data about the students themselves (test scores, demographics, attendance, etc.), as well as data about treatments or interventions intended to influence student outcomes. So, for example, professional development efforts aimed at improving the teaching of reading comprehension would need to be tracked, since these should have an impact on student learning. This implies that the school or instructor should collect the data locally and that the data should be used locally to inform teaching and targeted intervention programs. This is an important point that is often overlooked.

The most basic common unit of analysis (sometimes referred to as an atomistic unit) should drive data-collection efforts and processes. If the student is the smallest analytical entity that will be studied, then attributes of that entity should be collected. In schools, this means that data should be gathered at the source. If schools and classrooms are where learning is produced, then local teachers and administrators need to collect and understand the data that will be used to measure that learning. At the same time, however, districts need to integrate increasing demands for accountability, both fiscal and educational. Increasing scrutiny at the district level implies an entirely different focus for information system design. In this district accountability model, data are aggregated up to higher levels, such as the school or program, and are used to justify administrative or managerial decisions that affect large numbers of students and schools. This does not simply mean a reliance on central capacity. Knowledge management should be responsive to needs at all levels of the system. The problem is that the events and outcomes being monitored all tend to occur at the lowest levels of aggregation—the student.

Even in the most centralized system, instructional outcomes occur at the individual level. However, most district accountability measures and goals are aggregated to higher levels of the organization. Data on student and teacher absence, student program participation, teacher professional development activities and test scores need to be available at the lowest level for aggregation to any meaningful unit—classroom, grade, neighborhood, or other coherent grouping. This means that only individual-level data will serve. This is important because reform efforts must work on multiple levels. It is also vital that the system be transparent in order to combat efforts to cheat or otherwise tamper with the data. Data collected at the student or classroom level need to be aggregated and fed upwards to higher levels of the educational accountability structure to inform system decisions made at those levels. A system without proper security in place could be subject to manipulation by school-level actors. Again, this is not an argument for or against centralization, per se. Rather, one must recognize that there are knowledge management decisions that are appropriate and possible at each level of an organization. Data structures and analytical tools should reflect this reality.

This divergence between existing data systems and data needs points to a gap between new technological capabilities and the policy environment that would enable schools to actively collect relevant information and put it to use in a KM system. When the model of change targets student learning, it is essential to focus on identifying those innovations (technical and organizational) that best serve schools and classroom teachers. Most existing models of school governance do not provide for data analysis at the classroom level. Often there is also a gap between technical capacity and technical feasibility. Most educational systems have very little technical capacity. For example, teachers may not have easy access to the

Internet, or district computer staff may not have much experience supporting the analysis of problems relevant at the classroom level. There must be collection and delivery systems in place. There must also be analytical support for complex problems that are not solved by looking at simple bivariate comparisons.

Making instructional decisions in an individual classroom requires a sophisticated understanding of student attributes and of what individual curricular units can provide. The ability to generalize to a larger population is not a relevant concern in this context. At the school level, however, a principal may be very interested in how a new professional development activity is affecting student performance relative to other classes in the same building, or in comparison to other schools across the district that did or did not participate in the same training. The tools and data needed for within-classroom analysis are quite different from those necessary for a cross-school comparison. Differing forms of organizational analysis call for diverse forms of KM system implementation. One faces similar challenges at any level of aggregation, from the classroom through the district level to the federal level.

The lack of reliable data for school and student evaluation continues to be a vexing problem. Without a solid analytical model and the appropriate KM infrastructure to collect and aggregate the data, no district of any size would be able to implement a robust evaluation system. For example, many districts embrace an assessment policy that focuses on individual grade cohorts. This has led to the construction of information systems and testing plans that do not support longitudinal analysis of individual students. However, a system that allowed for accurate and fair evaluation at all levels of the educational system would differ radically from the current model that separates data use and evaluation (occurring at the state and district level) from the people who actually do the teaching and learning (schools, teachers, and students). A fair, consistent knowledge management system would provide an environment for implementing an appropriate stakes model at each level, rather than focusing high-stakes measures on teachers and children.

Organizational approaches

Differing organizational approaches to knowledge management are one of the most broadly discussed areas in the field. Much of the recent literature that seems to be relevant for KM is based on the study of complex commercial organizations—primarily large, multinational, financial, and high technology firms—and comes out of the major business schools in the United States and Europe. These studies of KM point to a number of issues that educational technologists must address in the design of school district information networks before we can make significant progress in areas that range from measuring individual student performance to the most demanding evaluations of large districts and state-level educational systems. The contributions of research on knowledge management to school and district can be applied most directly to strategic planning efforts. The Schools Interoperability Framework, and the National Center for Education Statistics all provide assistance in applying KM principles to planning and evaluation.

The organizational reform efforts can often best be described by the way in which they operationalize their KM strategies. There are four important dimensions of such strategies. New realities can be conceived of as both creating new services or goods and creating relationships with new customers. In this example, Organization A is an organisation that sees innovation in information technology as a way to reduce risks and costs. A school district following this strategy might implement a new in-school, computer-adaptive mathematics assessment to reduce outside testing costs and to help minimize instructional time lost to testing. Such a system might also help address the problem of mobile students who may not be included in once-a-year standard assessments. Such an assessment would be an element of a comprehensive program to reduce the risk of litigation associated with differential outcomes between poor and non-poor students by providing the opportunity to test adaptively and at smaller time intervals.

Organization B, on the other hand, perceives the value of improvements in information management as coming from adding value or enhancing existing interactions and creating new information services and products. A school following this strategy might invest in workgroup computers and a high-speed Internet connection. This technology would be used to support teaching a chemistry class in a virtual, web-based environment that would allow for the interaction of commercial and university subject-area experts as outside advisors and mentors for student projects. An effective organization with a well-designed information management plan will have a clear understanding of its place on these dimensions and will plan for its development needs accordingly. It seems clear that an organization with a mature understanding of the importance of information for decision-making might map its strategy as a circular structure, Organization C.

However, the costs involved in moving a complex organization along multiple axes simultaneously would almost certainly be prohibitive. It is important to recognize the tradeoffs between adding to and protecting what already exists.

Another dimension not explicitly captured in this graphic. Is a particular knowledge investment required for operation, is it essential for competition, or is it likely to bring distinction as a unique actor in the relevant market? Most investment in operational data systems tends to be directed toward the first two areas, day-to-day function and competition. It is the concept of standing out from the crowd that helps to drive truly innovative transformations of KM systems. In his research, Marchand finds that managers rarely say that significant portions of their investments are focused on applications that give them distinctive competencies with customers. The immediacy and relative clarity of an organization's current operational needs tend to drive most KM investment strategies. This is no less true for school districts. Any district will have a working payroll or bookkeeping system. There is no other alternative. These systems must be operational and deliver substantial value. Investments in long-term payoffs, such as those often encountered in improving educational systems, typically suffer by comparison. A system for tracking curriculum development and delivery is typically not characterized by a sense of urgency. The rationale for building such a system is less clear-cut than for the other, more traditional, operational data systems. Operational systems track and manage day-to-day transactions but are of little use for planning or evaluation purposes. However, as is the case with basic research in the manufacturing sectors, there needs to be substantial investment in a knowledge management infrastructure for any organization to reap long-term payoffs. The return on investment from knowledge is small in the short term but can have a huge impact in the long run.

The dimensional framework to schools and asks how information creates value in an educational setting, the level of analysis becomes extremely important. For example, one focus of a school district, because it performs the business functions of any large organisation system, would be on managing risks and reducing costs. District administrators would also be interested in producing increased learning, but they could only have an impact through indirect effects. One model of district action would be an active structuring of incentives and resources to create an environment in schools and classrooms that enhances learning. Bureaucratic structures are good at routine tasks and can provide infrastructure at a reasonable cost by taking advantage of economies of scale. Individual teachers, on the other hand, are engaged in directly adding value to the educational process and creating new realities for their students. This is a case of functional specialization. The problem is that actors at each of the levels need to be cognizant of the knowledge and system dynamics that define the other levels. Even within a district office, there will be differences across organizational boundaries. Curriculum support staff might be heavily focused on creating new realities by aligning district curricular resources with new standards or goals. This might include a training on demand streamed video system for delivering professional development when and where it suits individual teachers and coordinators. Using technology to overcome the boundaries of time and space can create many new opportunities.

A legal services team might be focused on reducing risk: for example, a district might put all Individualized

Educational Plans (IEPs) online with a system for tracking interventions and student performance. This might be one response to concerns that special education students are receiving uneven access to services. This system could provide both a tool for demonstrating compliance and encouraging school staff to stay on top of student needs by making school-level activities more transparent. This drastic over-simplification highlights the difficulties one encounters when trying to design a system that meets the needs of actors at multiple levels in the educational setting. It should be made clear that it is not necessary to build one monolithic knowledge management system. Indeed, it would be extremely difficult to build a complex system that would be adaptable enough to respond consistently to a changing educational policy environment.

A resource that has been developed in this regard is the Schools Interoperability Framework, which is an important acknowledgement of the heterogeneity of data-acquisition and knowledge- management systems in use today. Any realistic district information system must be made up of a matrix of interlocking systems that serve different functions and different user communities.

School districts are not unique in their spotty reliance on information technologies designed to enable and monitor reform efforts. Many district-level systems were created to comply with externally imposed reporting requirements. Unfortunately, investment in transformative types of information technology—technologies that will impact the underlying organizational goals and drastically expand capabilities—is inherently risky. In a recent study of large information technology.

Innovation in knowledge management is difficult in a complex organization. In education, we have long experience with the problem of differentiating direct and secondary effects. The expectation is that improvements in the educational setting—investments in class size reduction, teacher training, access to computers, etc.—will translate into improved learning on the part of the students. Schools and districts often engage in professional development efforts with the intent of improving student performance—an indirect effect of improving instruction. However, studies of the effectiveness of such efforts are often hampered by the difficulty of isolating and measuring the value added by a particular professional development program to performance at the individual student level. Expectations that simple technology initiatives will adequately address such complex problems are wildly optimistic, at best. Unrealistic expectations are as likely to be attached to smaller-scale applications of technology as they are to large technology systems.

One smaller-scale technological 'fix' that is frequently advocated is the availability of computers in classrooms. Computers are valuable tools and resources for both teachers and districts. However, what frequently goes unrecognized is that, in order to live up to the expectations and serve the needs of both teachers and district administrators, computers must become an integral part of the classroom environment. Technology used as just one more add-on activity will have very little educational impact other than perhaps increasing keyboarding skills. There must also be sufficient computing resources in the classroom with links to district-level data systems that allow individual teachers to make meaningful queries in real time. If one believes that frequent measurement is critical for gauging the value added by a particular educational strategy, the ability to record and evaluate data in real time is crucial. District or state level analysis, on the other hand, would be a centralized, top-down approach that would have little use for complex data structures and would only rely on school-level technology for acquiring data. This distinction in interest between consumers of data at the different organizational levels also reflects the need for a more global understanding of the importance of the timeliness of data collection and rapid turn-around for results that are to aid decision making at the classroom level.

The tension between district and classroom needs remains a troublesome barrier with respect to both turn-around time and the expected payoff for the time invested. Districts need data that are not immediately useful in the classroom (but must be collected there) and classroom teachers routinely assess their students and vary their interventions based on those assessments. Finally, there is a serious question about the validity of the measures of student learning used at both the school and district level. Teachers often question the alignment of standardized tests with enacted curricula. There are also concerns about the consequential validity of using such tests to make high-stakes decisions about the progress of students and the retention or pay of teachers. By the same token, while a classroom assessment may be valid within that classroom, the reliability of such measures is too low to be useful for comparing student progress within a school or across a district. This is a problem that technological innovations can address, but not in purely technical terms. The design of new assessment instruments may be enabled by new delivery and recording technologies. The rapid growth of computer-adaptive testing and its immediate scoring and reporting of results represent an enormous change from the typical 'fill in the bubble' examinations. Wide access to digital video has made the production of multimedia portfolios of student work a reality in many non-affluent schools. This is an area where the landscape is changing rapidly.

As distance technologies improve to allow teachers to collaborate with subject-area experts, master teachers, test constructors, and others, it will become easier to work together on test quality and comparability. The social organization of classroom support structures will need to change as well, but the hope for coordination at a higher conceptual level can be realized.

There has been a great deal written about new forms of technical infrastructure and about the role that enabling technologies play in knowledge management. Schools often have very little in the way of technological infrastructure on site. However, the current thinking about successful knowledge management warns against relying on technology to solve the whole data management problem. The importance of core technological capabilities is a myth developed by managers looking for stability in rapidly changing environments. Instead, she provides a list of non-technological characteristics of what she refers to as renewing (or successful) organizations, summarized as:

— *Enthusiasm for knowledge:* Knowledge seeking and accumulation are encouraged and rewarded. A spirit of inquiry drives people. Curiosity is seen as an important asset.

— *Staying ahead in knowledge:* Having the drive to continue to learn and expand capabilities. Anticipating customer needs is the focus—not responding to them.

— *Tight coupling of complementary skill sets:* Tear down internal boundaries and operate in teams. There need to be boundary spanners in each area to make these external connections—don't make everyone a generalist.

— *Iteration in activities:* Iterative improvements are the only constant. Developing core capabilities is more like gardening than building something—things need constant care and need to be turned under and replanted from time to time.

— *Higher order learning:* Don't just learn from operational needs. Listening too hard to current customers (problems, etc.) can blind one to the needs of potential customers in new markets.

— *Leaders who listen and learn:* Leaders at all levels need to be knowledgeable about the organization's technologies. Eager learners are the most effective managers.

The implications for many types of organizational culture. The points outlined above are entirely familiar to educators: Communities of learners can be described in this way. It is not surprising that the characteristics of successful teachers and teaching are similar to those necessary for success in other areas of professional interaction. However, it is essential that the importance of the level-of-analysis problem in this area be recognized as well. Information networks that link the different levels of educational innovation will encounter greater challenges to building interest and enthusiasm for knowledge if that knowledge is of little use at a particular level in the organization—especially if it is the level that must shoulder the greatest burden for data collection (i.e., the classroom). Likewise, there are difficulties in agreeing on data structures and analytical models when purposes differ. Questions focused on the performance of a particular third-grade reading program across a range of cohorts passing through that grade will engender datasets that are quite different from those created to answer questions about the long-term impact of that same program on a single cohort of students as they advance into higher grades. The data structures, analytical frameworks, and technological infrastructure necessary to answer questions in one area or level may have little relevance in another area or level. The importance of organizational culture for supporting knowledge management activities. It is also important to consider the involvement of critical users in the creations of a KM system.

The imperatives for successful implementation of information technology-based innovation from a different direction. They argue that users of a technology must be the focus of any development or change effort, not its target. For example, a centralised, system for student attendance might provide detailed output that is designed by a district staffer to satisfy a state reporting requirement. Local schools, however, might have multiple additional needs. This is often the case when technology is developed by a central bureaucracy to serve its own KM needs. A KM system for student assessment will look very different if a district office designs it for its own use from the way it would look if it had been designed by groups of classroom teachers to support instruction.

Traditional approaches to system development are too linear to adequately address the dynamic, multidimensional nature of successful knowledge management systems. Another important characteristic of successful KM projects is the presence of high-level non-information technology supporters (e.g., managers not in the technology or computer departments). Since the adoption of KM technology is largely a social process, it is vital that senior operational managers support the project and show that they value active participation. These caveats seem to be particularly important for projects that attempt to integrate the needs of multiple levels within an organization. High-level support that focuses on an overriding need—such as improving student test scores—can be very effective in overcoming traditional barriers to cooperation that are often encountered in bureaucratic organizations. Needs that can be defined more broadly—that appeal to organization-wide norms or goals—are best articulated from upper levels of management and have the best chance of being widely accepted if they are sponsored by someone with no parochial interest in one system or another. Others have addressed the problem of integrating human and technical systems.

Technology is important for efficient transfer of vital knowledge, but delivers its benefits only as it supports human communication and knowledge construction. O'Dell and her colleagues also provide important insights about some general rules-of-thumb for KM systems. They argue that the more valuable the knowledge, the less sophisticated the technology that supports it". For example, large data warehouses and data mining tools typically yield low-value knowledge, while a low-tech help desk delivers high-value knowledge. This is the difference between looking at pages of tabular data on the one hand and statistical analysis and advice from an expert on the other. The expert brings personal experience, context sensitivity, and technical skill and combines it with the data at hand to produce integrated knowledge as an output. The important point of this example is that the expert interprets information—data that has been systematized. It is the aggregation of information and expertise that produces knowledge. The low-tech/high-tech split reflects the fact that tacit knowledge is best shared through people; explicit knowledge can be shared through machines. Or, the more tacit the knowledge, the less high-tech the solution.

District-level information systems often contain a great deal of explicit knowledge about students and schools. Tacit knowledge is that uncodified knowledge that is based on personal experience, absorption of organizational norms, and other factors. Explicit knowledge is information that has been written down or recorded in an information system. This might seem like a simplistic distinction, but it has important implications for decision-making and the reform process. This does not mean that the accumulation and transmission of tacit knowledge is not possible. Rather, it means that knowledge management systems must have imbedded in them some portion of the critical tacit knowledge needed to interpret information in the system at hand. For instructional decisions, teachers and school-level administrators, for example, often operate on the basis of tacit knowledge about an individual student or group of students. These data are much more difficult to aggregate and transfer.

The primary problem is not technical. Rather, it is the difficulty of developing relevant metrics for a wealth of anecdotal data. Another important example of the importance of tacit knowledge is the practice of using individuals as the focal point of reform efforts. School districts often use successful principals and other administrators as agents of change. Administrators that have been able to turn a school around are seen as a valuable commodity. The literature on KM refers to this process as one of using mobile intellectual capital to bring expert skill to bear on a particular local problem. The value of intellectual capital is often the tacit knowledge about how one manages curricular changes or fosters a positive school climate. This process of conveying tacit knowledge about such a complex task is one example of a knowledge system. The drawback is that tacit data is not easily transferred and successes at one location are not easily replicable to another.

Some KM system-designers attempt to imbed the interpretation of experts in the outputs of the system; for example, one might present a bar graph of mean scores on a particular set of assessments. A more knowledge-rich presentation might include a representation of error bands around the mean, or provide a comparison to scores of the same students in a prior assessment. It is not merely that the information presented should be contextualised. It is important that the contextualization be done in a way that makes a valid comparison and enhances the explanatory power of the measure in question. There are distinctions along the continuum from data to knowledge.

The data structures in this case must be available at the individual level and be sufficiently broad for meaningful diagnostic use. Making the linkages clear between different levels of the organization and building methods of capturing and using tacit knowledge are two characteristics that must remain in the forefront of any design effort.

Much of the work that went into this paper was informed by nearly eight years of experience working with education assessment and program data from the Milwaukee Public Schools (MPS). It has become increasingly clear that the ability of complex educational agencies to perform timely, in-depth, and accurate analysis is severely hampered by data-access problems. Indeed, there are increasing concerns that the district does not have the data it needs to make many important decisions or, if the data exists, they resides in a computer system that is difficult to use. In our work with MPS, we hope to take advantage of two major ongoing efforts. The first is the Schools Interoperability Framework (SIF). The initial area of collaboration will be in the area of intra-application communication. The model the SIF group is supporting is an open-system environment. This approach recognizes that schools and districts will continue to use a mix of information technologies from various vendors. The SIF initiative is focused on setting data exchange standards that will let the major school management and instructional support packages talk to each other without human mediation. This will help to decrease the transaction costs of systems with broader functionality and should allow for better aggregation of data across schools, districts, and states.

The founders of the SIF emphasise the need for comprehensive, consistent data management from a market-driven point of view. They argue that it is impossible to provide sophisticated applications if each individual school district pursues its own data-management strategy. The challenge the SIF has set for itself is based on the efforts of the business information technology community to move from data-management to knowledge-management systems. While the issues involved in successful knowledge management are largely absent in the literature on educational administration and assessment, an important and growing body of work is emerging from business schools around the world. These works range from thinking about the role of experts in organizational learning to multi-dimensional representations of the lifecycle of knowledge.

The Financial Times recently ran a three-month series reviewing the current thinking in academia about knowledge-management systems. The second important strand of work comes from the National Center for Education Statistics. This effort produced a comprehensive, standards-based model for school data system definitions. Unlike a product created by a particular vendor, district-level, state-level, and federal education administrators developed this model. Rather than being market-driven, the NCES Forum on Educational Statistics focused on the decision-making needs of school- and district-level administrators. This focus on users of data turns the traditional approach on its head. Most major school software systems—such as the offerings for National Computer Systems (NCS)—are driven by a lowest-common-denominator approach, where the package provides for the minimum needs for the maximum number of possible users. The NCES data elements, on the other hand, are developed to a high level of specificity and are intended to be extremely flexible and encompass the widest possible use. Both of these efforts point toward the importance of standardized acquisition and the use of data for day-to-day and long-range decision making.

The issue of standardisation is particularly important when the focus is on evaluation. Increasing demands by outside funders and state and local agencies for data on program impact continue to raise the analytical burden placed on the district. In traditional transactional student data systems, the focus is on managing schedules and tracking attendance and grades. Reporting is designed using a top-down approach that is focused on district, state, and federal reporting requirements. What the NCES proposes is a much more flexible design that would support very fine-grained inquiry from any level of the organization.

Knowledge management is such a wide-open area of study that it is difficult to understand the implications of these models of knowledge management for an educational setting. One thing seems certain. School information systems are one of the most difficult to harness because they often lack any overall rationality for. cooperation and compliance. Differences in data needs and uses across different organizational levels present significant barriers to the collaboration necessary for innovation in knowledge management.

The Data Warehouse is also several years behind schedule. There remain two major stumbling blocks to the development and use of the system. The first hurdle is the difficulty of producing assessment, enrollment, and program participation statistics that match those created by the existing combination of mainframe exports, SAS (statistical software) scripting, and hand manipulation used to produce the district's accountability reports. This problem can be traced back to the inherent complexity of the analytical puzzle of tracking a highly mobile population of students with an archaic information system that relies on a great deal of expert knowledge on the part of its users. This is simply a high-dimensional analytical problem that cannot be easily moved from one system to another.

The other problem is that the new data system uses different data element definitions, field layouts, and formats. The new system is designed to take into consideration the improvements in methodology and changes in how one defines important school metrics such as value-added assessment and program effectiveness. Any comparison of analytical models between the two methods of producing accountability statistics requires the ability to engage in a sophisticated translation among approaches that are vastly different. The other stumbling block the Data Warehouse faces is the method of access that school administrators and teachers will use to extract data for local analysis.

The tool that was initially adopted is being used by district-level analysts in the Department of Technology Services and the Office of Research and Assessment, but was seen as too complicated for the average or casual user. Other solutions that rely on Web-based access are either not supported by the some of the desktop technologies in place, do not meet the security requirements the district must meet to protect student data, or are as complex as the tool the district is currently using. Finally, the lack of strategic planning and strategic resource allocation continues to plague development efforts at the district level. It is possible to raise funds to support the infrastructure in providing high-speed video to several thousand classrooms, but it is difficult to find the resources to train the staff to use video effectively, or to build an evaluation system to track the impact of this technology on teaching and learning.

Fair Use in Teaching

The Doctrine of Fair Use was conceived by the courts. It exempts certain categories of activity in some instances from the legal obligation to obtain permission from the author of a work before copying, performing, or displaying that work. Potentially exempt activities include teaching, research, scholarship, reporting, commentary, and even parody. The justification for the Fair Use exemption derives from the court's view that sometimes free and open discourse about ideas can be more of a stimulant to creation of new knowledge and new creative works than protection of the author's ability to reap financial reward from his work.

Traditionally the use of excerpts from copyrighted materials for classroom teaching has been conceived as a Fair Use. In 1976 the U.S. Congress formally adopted the Doctrine of Fair Use into its revision of the Copyright Act. That was twenty-five years ago. Since then technologies for reproducing, copying and displaying copyrighted materials have changed dramatically, and the locus for teaching activities has expanded beyond the classroom to include the airwaves (as in educational TV) and now the Internet. These changes have affected authors', teachers', and publishers' perspectives about is "fair" and what is not "fair."

Today as the educational community moves rapidly towards web-based education and a growing emphasis on distance learning, we believe it is important to take a another look at Fair Use and its relationship to evolving instructional technologies, if only to protect schools, teachers, and course developers from unexpected legal challenges.

First, however, to understand Fair Use and its application to education, one must give up any idea that "fair use" was ever really about equity. It's not. Like copyright itself, the doctrine derives ultimately from Western concepts of individualism and principles of market- based capitalism. The identification of what is "fair" or "not fair" is deeply entwined with the nature and ownership of the technologies used to reproduce or distribute the works in question as well as to who stands to gain or loose from a particular type of use.

The basis for copyright is established by Article 1, Section 8.h of the United States Constitution, which states: "The Congress shall have power to promote the progress of science and useful arts by securing for limited times to authors and inventors the exclusive right to their respective writings and discoveries." Copyright (along with patent, trade secret, and trademark) is the tool that implements the Constitutional purpose.

Copyright is a legally enforceable intellectual property right that protects a financial incentive designed to encourage individuals to take the risk of creating new works or improving on previous ones. The productivity and innovation that lie at the heart of US economic success seems to provide clear testimony for the wisdom of the framers of the Constitution..

Before the Copyright Revision Act of 1976, the record of cases involving Fair Use of copyrighted material in the classroom is sparse. What exists draws on the general principle that copying for classroom use without obtaining permission from the author was not an infringement of copyright as long as there was no impact on the sale of published books or sheet music.

There were only two cases concerning classroom copying by instructors before 1976. Both addressed the question of what portion of a copyrighted work could be freely copied and distributed to students under the Doctrine of Fair Use. The earliest of these, Macmillan Co. v. King 223 Fed. 862, was brought against a Harvard tutor who produced for his students very detailed outlines and summaries of an economics textbook published by Macmillan.

Macmillan argued this was an infringement of copyright and negatively impacted their market. Although most students did purchase the classroom text, some did not, apparently relying solely on their tutor's materials. The court ruled against the tutor. In the next case, Withol v. Crow 309 F.2d. 778th Cir. 1962, fifty years later, the court similarly ruled against a music teacher, who, short by forty-eight copies of a musical score for his students, decided to make copies rather than purchase additional scores from the publisher.

These two cases represent essentially all of the case law defining the application of Fair Use to teaching activities until the 1976 Copyright Revision Act. Clearly it did seem at that point that if a teacher stayed safely below some upper limit of copying an entire work, then the teacher would not risk a complaint that her activity was not Fair Use.

After 1976, however, Fair Use became more complicated for teachers. Even as the Congressional revision generally identified copying for educational purposes a potentially Fair Use, it laid a foundation for confusion by setting forth criteria to use in the determination of whether or not a specific instance of copying was actually a Fair Use.

Section 107 specifically states that making multiple copies of copyrighted materials for use in a classroom is not in itself an infringement of copyright. It then defines four factors that are to be used to analyze any specific situation—and so enters uncertainty: In determining whether the use made of a work in any particular case is a fair use the factors to be considered shall include:

— the purpose and character of the use, including whether such use is of a commercial nature or is for nonprofit education purposes;

— the nature of the copyrighted work;

— the amount and substantiality of the portion used in relation to the copyrighted work as a whole; and the effect of the use upon the potential market for or value of the copyrighted work.

— In interpreting this section, the courts thus far have generally viewed the forth factor, potential market impact, as the most important factor, given that the commercial and financial monopoly is at the heart of the concept of copyright. However, the use of the word "includes" rather than "are" in this section opens the door to a suggestion that there could be other factors, perhaps more important, influencing the interpretation of a particular situation.

Section 110, establishes that Fair Use may apply to performance or display of copyrighted works during "face-to-face teaching activities" that are "a regular part of the systematic instructional activities of a government body or a nonprofit educational institution." The language here seems to focus on making a careful distinction between what might be construed as Fair Use for educational purposes and some other use that might be construed as either "entertainment" or a commercially motivated performance or display.

The limitation of non-infringing performances to only those used in "face-to-face teaching activities" and the introduction of the vague concept that the non-infringing performance must be "integrated into a systematic course of instruction" further increase the complexity of applying this doctrine in the contemporary educational environment where digital instructional technologies allow teachers to download audio, video, graphics, text, photography, and radio and TV-like "webcasts" and "display" them to students inside or outside the traditional classroom via a class website.

The Congressional Record reveals that there was some real disagreement between those stakeholders interested in maintaining copyright free from any significant educational entitlements and the academic community which views Fair Use for education purposes as an historic privilege. Educators on the committee also argued that teachers should be excused from obtaining permissions because the very process of obtaining and paying royalties to use materials would be an onerous duty and an inhibitor of academic freedom. Indeed, the guidelines are very conservative and are increasingly difficult to apply in practice.

Part of the reason they sound so silly today is that in being so specific they have simply not kept pace with changes in copying technologies (photocopying and computers). The guidelines set a very constrained standard for what may be construed as a "Fair Use" in an educational setting and may appear to contradict a more expansive interpretation of the language in the statute itself. For example, the guidelines define "brevity" as not more than 250 words of poetry, or 2500 words or less from a complete article, short story or essay, or 1000 words or 10 percent (whichever is less) from any prose work.. Copies of these brief excepts are non-infringing only if they are also "spontaneous" (i.e., according to the guidelines, a last-minute inspiration of the teacher) and one-time.

According to authors of the guidelines, the basis for an exemption for such spontaneous one-time use of copyrighted works was simply to allow teachers enough time to obtain permission for the next classroom use (a process that in the mid-1970s took from four to eight weeks). Lost is the court's concept in the original doctrine of Fair Use that there was general social benefit in open discourse which itself was an encouragement of new ideas and innovation. The guidelines make clear that any post-class distributions of teaching materials to an interested but non-registered student could never be construed as Fair Use. The danger of teachers seriously impacting revenues from the sale of books and periodicals by making copies on the departmental mimeograph machines probably seemed fairly remote even to the teachers themselves. Indeed, in practice many teachers may have felt the constraints of the guidelines tight but livable given the situation. Anyway, it was standard teaching practice at that time, particularly in colleges and universities, was to send the students to the library reserved reading room.

The American Association of University Professors and the Association of Law Schools joined in arguing that the guidelines failed to take into account the reality of how teachers actually used materials for teaching purposes. They argued, more to the point, To protect themselves, many Universities today still disseminate the 1976 guidelines to their faculties, probably with tongue deeply embedded in cheek.

The photocopy revolution came in after 1976. With it libraries and instructors had a means to quickly, easily, and cheaply reproduce quantities of materials for research and teaching. Instead of gathering books and journals onto the shelves of the reserved book room where students lined up to read assignments from the one or two available copies, libraries and instructors could just hit the "number of copies" button on a big machine and in minutes have copies for even the largest class. The old departmental mimeograph machine went to salvage and a typical student excuse for not doing the reading disappeared. Instructors also felt themselves freer to pick and choose reading material for their students without being bound by selections in someone else's textbook.. Commercial copy centers sprang up around campuses, reserve reading rooms dimmed their lights, and the "coursepack" was born.

Meanwhile publishers and authors saw the photocopy machine as creating a whole new market for the sale of rights to reprint portions of books and articles from journals. Two cases established the rules for determining Fair Use in this new technical environment. The first was Basic Books v. Kinko's 758 F. Supp. 1522. In this case the publisher, Basic Books, challenged Kinko's failure to obtain permission from the copyright holders (usually the publishers) when reproducing coursepacks.

Although Kinko's argued that permission was not needed because the coursepacks were for classroom use and hence were exempt under Fair Use, the court agreed with Basic Books. Kinko's had unfortunately attracted the attention of the publishing world by advertising its ability to produce quick turn around of copies because it did not have to take the time to obtain permission from publishers. An analysis of the Kinko's case emphasizes the commercial nature of copyright law and demonstrates how the Doctrine of Fair Use may be modified when a new technology creates opportunities for business.

The court held that Kinko's failure to obtain permission had negatively impacted the market in permission or licensing fees. Kinko's had "extinguished" a financial reward to the copyright holder (the publisher), which was precisely the reward that copyright was designed to protect. Today most copy shops rigorously refuse to reproduce coursepacks unless permission to reprint has been granted in writing. Any permission fees charged by the copyright owner are then passed on to the students.

The key to understanding the Kinko's case is to see that the court did not really address the Doctrine of Fair Use as it applies to actions by instructors and students. Instead, with typical narrowness, the court focused the discussion entirely on the two businesses in the middle of that educational relationship. Since the copy shop had a commercial interest in the coursepack, the copy shop could not view its own reproduction as "Fair Use," despite the end use of its product for classroom teaching purposes.

The principle laid down in Basic Books v. Kinko's was repeated, clarified, and perhaps strengthened in a second case on the same issue: Princeton University Press v. Michigan Document Services 99F.3d. 1381. In this case, Michigan Document was one among several copy shops operating near campus. Its owner deliberately set out to test the ruling in the 1991 Basic Books case. Michigan Document therefore, not only did not obtain permission to reproduce materials for coursepacks, but also advertised this action, passed the savings incurred on to students, and used this reduction in price to undercut competitors. It is not surprising Michigan Document drew the attention of the publishers, and a negative ruling from the court.

The court reaffirmed that if the copier makes money from the copying, then the copying could not be construed to be Fair Use, even though the reproduction had an ultimate educational purpose. The court amplified that the Fair Use exemption is not a blanket exemption and that when litigants have commercial interests, the burden of proof that a copying situation is "fair" lies with the copier—in this case the copy shop. Since ultimately the copy shop is in the business of commerce, that is in making money not in teaching, the Doctrine of Fair Use does not apply.

The court also again noted the existence of a lucrative new market in permissions created by photocopy technology. Teachers who believe they can "get around" the commercial aspect of the copyshop decisions by making their own copies in the library or on their own office copy machines might do well to take another look at the story of the Harvard tutor back in 1914. The court has never actually tested the legitimacy of the coursepack itself, just of its reproduction by a commercial business.

Essentially the coursepack is a unique collection of materials assembled by an instructor for a particular class that may be delivered one or more times. Components of the "pack" are quite long—whole chapters, articles, essays, or stories—far exceeding the so called safe harbor standards presented in the classroom guidelines. Under the 1976 Act such a collection itself is a copyrightable work, referred to as a "collective work."

The digital technology for both desk-top publishing and distance learning, including webcasting, class web-sites, e- learning, and in-class real-time Internet access, is here now here. With it has come a quantum leap in the murkiness of applying the Doctrine of Fair Use for education. Not only does the approach suggested by the 1976 Act seem outdated, but also Congress's recent effort to update copyright for the computer age—the 1998 Digital Millennium Copyright Act—deliberately sidesteps many of the toughest issues for educators by declaring them simply "unsettled." The first "unsettled"—if not "unsettling"—issue concerns the definition "copy" on the Internet.

According to the Copyright Act, to be a "copy" the reproduced work needs only to be fixed in a tangible medium of expression. In Advanced Computer Services v. MAI Systems Corp., 845 F. Suppl. 356, the court ruled "the representation created in the RAM 'is sufficiently permanent or stable to permit it to be perceived, reproduced, or otherwise communicated for a period of more than transitory duration'."

Although the focus of Advanced Computer Services was software, the principle laid down by that decision would seem to be applicable to any work, including articles and Power Point presentations, or video clips, viewed or read via the Internet. If that is so, it raises the spectre of every single viewing of copyrighted materials over the Internet involving either a potential copyright infringement or a royalty payment.

This interpretation seems overly restrictive, undercutting the balancing of interests that copyright law attempts to achieve between public and private benefits. While authors do need protection of their ability to reap benefits both in dollars and reputation, the ultimate goal of copyright—the encouragement and advancement of knowledge and creativity—would not be served by skewing everything in the direction of the author's monopoly of copyright. Indeed, the court in Religious Technology Center v. Netcom On-Line Communications Services. Inc., 907 F. Supp. 1361 took a more reasonable approach when it characterized what happens when a user browses through materials on the Internet as "the functional equivalent reading"—not copying.

Judge Whyte viewed this such reproduction of a file on the computer screen as simply a necessity for humans to perceive the information—rather like stand-up reading in a book store or borrowing a journal from the library. We hope, in the end, that Judge Whyte's reasonable view will prevail. Anti-copying technology certainly exists to disable a reader's ability to print, attach, or email an article over the Internet—activities that may be closer to a traditional understanding of copying. However, such distinctions are by no means without uncertainty in the evolving legal environment.

How, then, will the Fair Use Doctrine be applied to education and teaching in this environment? Unfortunately, current trends appear to be towards protecting commercial interests rather than protecting the public's access to knowledge or learning. We note that the instructor and the learner in any on-line situation are often separated by one or many commercial interests—for example an Internet service providers (ISPs) or an e-business providing course management or courseware to an instructor. One would do well to recall the Kinkos and the Michigan Document decisions.

In addition, technology may help resolve the complaint made in the minority report on the classroom guidelines that the task of obtaining permission to use copyrighted materials is onerous and time consuming. This, at any rate, is one possible implication to be derived from the decision in American Geophysical Union v. Texaco, 802 F. Supp. 1. In this case the court ruled against a Texaco researcher who, for his own convenience, regularly made photocopies of articles from journals which he kept in his office for future reference. Though such copying is common practice among both researchers and teachers, whether working in commercial or noncommercial context, the court accepted the copyright owner's argument that permissions were easy to get because of new Internet-based Copyright Clearinghouse technology and then went on to reason that since the ultimate purpose of the researcher's activity was profit for his employer (Texaco) that the private monopoly interest of the authors should prevail.

Somewhere the larger issue that led to the establishment of the Doctrine of Fair Use in the first place seems to have gotten lost in excitement over how easy the new technology can make the payments for copying rights flow. We as a society need to stop a moment and review what earlier courts had to say about the importance of support for the individual teacher or researcher who is exploring ideas and creating knowledge for the next generation and the general benefit of society. The current use of Internet technology to support teaching brings new commercial players into the communications continuum, separating teacher and student in the so-called distance learning environment.

6

Towards Education Virtually

New information technologies are opening the system to new possibilities as surely as new building technologies did to architecture some hundred years ago. But the technologies do not design new practices for human being. People, acting in the face of uncertainty, must determine what they can make of these emerging possibilities.

Many groups and interests, pursuing many divergent inspirations, are vying for command, and a kaleidoscope of coalitions establishes, through diverse initiatives, emerging norms of practice.

Many in journalism and commerce avidly attend to the entertainment industries as potential sources of educational innovation. They may be right in viewing practitioners of edutainment--the merger of education and entertainment in products, at once enlightening and engaging, to be marketed to both homes and schools--as the key groups that determine emerging pedagogical prospects.

Significant limitations to these efforts to restructure educational practice through edutainment are at work, however. Edutainment's stuff in trade is a set of products to be sold in the educational markets of home and school. Indubitably, schools and teachers and students, engaged in the work of education, constitute a market for the sale of various goods--food, books, clothes, pens and pencils, furniture, fuel oil, rings, electronics, and software.

Education as such, however, is not inherently a market, with success measured in market share and relative efficiency in making and distributing product. Many a fool has emerged from a richly financed education, and many others have earned hard wisdom through a sparse regimen of study. As a human phenomenon, education is not a market for products, but a process of growth and transformation, one sustained over many years with success measured throughout the vicissitudes of personal and collective experience.

Indeed, many companies may do well by doing good. But producers of edutainment have yet to show whether they have either an interest in the human process of education or the capacity to give it intentional shape. Surely the activities of such companies, like those of mass communicators throughout the 20th century, will have significant effects on the cultural context within which educational work takes place. But the likelihood is slim that the producers of edutainment, as such and single-handedly, will be the prime reshapers of the processes of education.

Education is the work of educators, not movie producers, broadcasters, or theme-park operators. Educational institutions--schools, universities, museums, laboratories, libraries--are the major factors in the social construction of a new educational system. Worldwide they control a huge annual cash flow, derived from individual, governmental, philanthropic, and commercial sources, a cash flow more than sufficient to underwrite far-flung innovation.

Furthermore, they control and produce intellectual property of extraordinary breadth and depth. The holdings of Hollywood are but a pittance compared to those of the world's universities, laboratories, museums, and libraries, and the changes wrought by the digital technologies are making those very holdings more accessible, productive, and meaningful in the lives of everyone.

When people talk about the fruits of intellectual work at its higher levels, they generally think of forms of knowledge spread across an intellectual spectrum that runs from universal scholarship--pure achievements of disinterested reflection--to the domains of professional practice--applied principles of organized performance.

Across every field, education included, people need both pure scholarship and professional learning. An agenda for reconstructing the educational system will touch both the academic and the professional and occupy all the intervening space. Intellectual work involves action of the burdensome sort in which thought guides the effort. If, from the perspective of intellectual institutions, a spectrum running from pure to applied, from academic to professional, characterizes knowledge, then a gradient running from theory to policy to practice generally describes the intellectual and educational uses to which people put that knowledge. Sometimes theory guides work and activity; other times policy controls it; and often patterns of practice shape action. Properly speaking, these are ideal types, like the poles of pure academic knowledge and applied professional learning. As ideal types they are intellectual formulations applied to the stuff of experience, not empirical actualities substantially involved in it.

To make a shift in the spectrum of pedagogical possibility clear, consider the history of architecture in the hundred years from 1850 or so. Until that time, throughout history and across cultures people simply did not build tall buildings except for a few towers for specialized ceremonial and military purposes. Then a series of innovations occurred, for reasons quite extraneous to the will of architects, that made unprecedented structures feasible. With new materials like structural steel, reinforced concrete, and plate glass, with new techniques for managing water, heat, light, and air, and with novel ways of moving people, these unprecedented structures proved so humanly habitable that specimens of them have been built the world around, with great variations of form and function and with diverse triumphs and failures on all sorts of measures--social, structural, economic, and aesthetic. The new building technologies did not determine, in a strong sense, how any particular city would look, but they did open a wide new spectrum of architectural possibility. Within the range of this possibility numerous cities have developed imposing skylines like New York's; even Paris, by explicitly adhering to traditional building codes in its central sections, reflects through its conscious restraint one of the possibilities of the new architecture.

Digital technologies are for education as iron and steel girders, reinforced concrete, plate glass, elevators, central heating, and air conditioning were for architecture. Digital technologies set in abeyance significant, long-lasting limits on educational activity. High-speed, wide-area networks linking ubiquitous computers to copious digital libraries transform the cultural conditions under which educational interactions take place. Traditionally, the school and the classroom have been places where teachers and students are isolated from the general culture and where information and ideas have been relatively scarce -- the textbook is a meager selection of what a field of knowledge comprises, a skilled teacher is a bundle of ignorance relative to the sum of learning, and a school library a sparse collection at best. Networks reaching through the school into the classroom and to the desktop are ending the isolation and substituting a rule of abundance for that of scarcity.[Note 2] Such a new rule is not without its pitfalls, but to cope with these we must recognize that it is a new rule, deeply different from the old. In our extended present, the educational problem changes profoundly, shifting from determining strategies for disbursing scarce knowledge to finding ways to enable people to use unlimited access to the resources of our cultures.

New media alter the ways of knowing and the opportunities for participating in the creation of knowledge. Multimedia, and its extension in virtual reality, is not merely a glitzy vehicle for edutainment hype. It is an epistemologically interesting development in our culture. For the most part, the work of thought has seemed to take place primarily through the manipulation of language, with the formal symbolization of mathematics and logic seen as extensions of more everyday linguistic forms. Multimedia make it increasingly evident that the work of thinking can take many forms -- verbal, visual, auditory, kinetic, and blends of all and each. Of course, nonlinguistic media are not new, but their status as serious means for creating knowledge is rising considerably. Knowledge consists primarily of cultural resources that people can store and retrieve on demand, as the need for it arises. Written, especially printed, media long held a privileged place in education because they were easy to store and retrieve to suit the needs of users. Work in other media tended to exist in performances and monuments, which did not suit the strategies of random access. Multimedia changes that condition. It subjects a far wider range of communications to the full rule of random access, changing the repertoire of resources that people can store and retrieve effectively and use on demand to serve the needs of disciplined thought and inquiry.People can use digital media both to acquire ideas and to express their thoughts in diverse ways. As a result, educators will find it increasingly difficult to favor the linguistic modality over all others, and they will need to broaden the norms of academic excellence.

Digital technologies expand personal potentialities. Distributed processing and ubiquitous computing may or may not aggregate into artificial intelligence in the strong sense, creating a species of machines that think in a significant way. But they are clearly coming to function as a means for augmenting our human intellectual skills. Word processors warn of anomalous spellings as they occur; spreadsheets allow anyone to perform complex calculations quickly and accurately; and databases permit those with good memory or bad to manage information sets that neither could handle on his own. All sorts of more specialized tools greatly lower the skill levels needed to participate effectively in wide ranges of cultural activity. Precision and exactness may become trivial proficiencies because getting it right will be easy, provided one doesn't get it wildly wrong through some accidental error. With regard to such accidental but sometimes very portentous error, the ability to estimate and guess results, traditionally an educationally suspect knack, becomes an increasingly prized skill. Thus, educators are sensing that changes in information technologies can deeply transform the hallmarks of having acquired a decent education. Established answers to the question "What knowledge is of most worth?" may not pertain under the conditions of learning and knowing that emerge with the digital augmentation of human intelligence.

Digital libraries, multimedia, and augmented skills change the limits of educational practice. This proposition is not a prediction, but an observation about the potentialities inherent in communications innovations taking place in our extended present. The basic proposition here is not so much a normative argument that educators should, for one or another reason, accept that these three developments are empowering the transformation of educational activity. Rather, the proposition is more factual, although tentative.

As educators experience changing conditions of communication in their work, they understand that these developments are profoundly altering the spectrum of pedagogical possibility. Individual educators may or may not welcome that condition, but critic and evangelist alike sense that the new conditions open the educational system to significant change. The new conditions, however, do not determine what will emerge. Educators are determining what emerges through the social construction of digital learning communities. Educational structures from kindergarten through graduate schools and adult education are increasingly in flux. Structures are wrenching open to change; but the course that change can and should take must be determined through the interplay of effort by many different groups.

ICT Tools for Education

The singular technological feature, which is a turning point for ICTs, is the pre-eminence of the Internet Protocol (IP) for communication, around which ICTs are reorienting and growing. This versatile connectionless protocol is a method by which data is sent over the Internet as packets from one computer to another, each having a unique address. Different packets may be delivered through different routes to their destination, where they are resequenced by the Transmission Control Protocol (TCP) and put back in the right order. The Wide Area Networks (WAN) which are identified as Internet (international networks), Intranets (corporate or intra-organizational networks) and Extranets (extra-organizational networks) are all IP-based. IP has left its imprint not only on Metropolitan Area Networks (MAN) and Local Area Networks (LAN), but also on equipment such as the network computer, workstation, work group server, media server, Web server, cable TV networks, wireless 'last mile link' to the customer premises, set-top-box and even a kiosk.

Computer Software

Technologies driving the content market have brought about new developments which have increased the speed, capacity and versatility of computer hardware.

Moore's Law has predictably doubled the performance of microprocessors every 18 months and personal computers (PCs) have become increasingly powerful with the introduction of new devices such as cache, more effective architecture and bus interfaces as well as extensive instruction sets.

The introduction of the Slot-1 interface in the second generation of the Intel Pentium family of chips, from the first generation 296-pin Socket-7 interface, made a 242-Contact Slot Access available through a cartridge with a single edge contact. This innovation will ensure a smooth upgrading from one model of the chip to the next without having to change the PC design extensively. The result is a designer's paradise for minimizing user problems, while upgrading the capacity of PCs frequently to accommodate an ever-growing range of content.

The low cost medium speed entry-level Covington allows designers to create a plethora of product lines from a single mother board. Mendocino is increasing the 128K of L-2 Cache on the processor chip at processor speeds. The Celeron chip has the capacity to produce further growth in the content market. The three leading chip manufacturers, AMD, Cyrix and IDT, are marketing K6, MXi and C6 chips respectively in competition with Intel, and will strengthen their position by early 1999 with the introduction of K7, Jalapeno and C7. By then, Intel will be expanding its processing capacity with Katmai and Merced Chips with a 64-Bit instruction set for the server and workstation markets.

Hand-held computing is becoming a useful tool for the collection of data in the field. Battery-operated receptacles of wireless information, integrated PDA chips like Intel's Strong Arm-1100 running at 200 MHz consuming only 200 milliwatts to power a hand-held PC, 3Com's Palm-III with an infrared receiver and wired modem for connecting to the Web, and Novatel Minstrel's Wireless Modem, which integrates both data and voice communication, are forerunners in this area.

Optical Read Only Memory (OROM), with up to 128 MB of storage and no moving parts, provides extra storage in the hand-held PC. Philips Nino Palm PC which runs pocket versions of Microsoft applications is already available, although the battery power pack at present does not last for more than a few weeks. A close competitor, Windows CE, is gaining momentum.

The main problem in home automation is the communication among various devices and appliances. A possible solution appeared with several technologies using existing home are wiring for telephone, and computer and appliance control utilizing the X-10 Standard module available for most types of appliances. Consumer electronics and PC industry companies have also agreed upon a new consumer electronics bus standard (LE bus), marketed, for instance, by Home Plug and Play, which is an improvement on the X-10 standard followed previously. Software for controlling modules of either of these standards is available. Ethernet PC network with CE-Bus controllers can be connected to PCs and home entertainment systems.

The desk top Sedona offers a versatile tool for content searching which groups file system, Web browser and e-mail client into a single graphic user interface - a trendsetting concept developed by the Intel Architecture Lab (IAL). Sedona can locate items selectively and find files, e-mail, Web pages or news items of interest without any active input. It can also correlate a message or a document that has been opened with other relevant stored information.

New audio standards have been introduced which allow multimedia to provide real-life, 3-D sound for content developers of titles encoded with Dolby digital. This can add depth to sound, almost to the point of immersion. Multimedia titles can now be encoded with information that creates the illusion of 3-D sound with just headphones or a pair of PC speakers. Direct sound and Direct sound 3-D from Microsoft allows for the mixing of multiple audio streams and programme-surround channels.

As multimedia require larger and larger files, the 1.44 M B capacity of the floppy disk is becoming less appealing and is giving way to three typical competing technologies for removable drive: IOMEGA Zip Drive, Sony-Fujifilm HiFd and LS-120, tending towards the goal of inexpensive 100 MB adequate for multimedia presentation applications, and of course compatible with the existing 3.5 inch floppy disks.

There is a shift from compact disc-read only memory (CD-ROM), towards digital versatile disc read-only memory, version 2 (DVD-ROM-2) drives which can read CD recordable or CD rewritable media. Though better than DVD-ROM-1, at present, they lag behind the fastest CD-ROM drives in overall performance.

The sheer enormity of DVD capacity will be useful for storing raw data. It is possible to make feature-length, documentary films using DVD, using high-resolution MPEG-2-standard video compression, immersive Dolby-standard audio compression and extensive 3-D graphics. Everything from high density needs to theatre quality audio and video has become possible. Compared to the 650 MB peak capacity of CD-ROM, contemporary DVD-ROM media can store nearly 5 G B of data per side, and this quantity will soon attain 1 7 G B. MPEG-2 has now surpassed the quality of laser disks. An interactive geographic Map Atlas, giving a terrain database of the entire surface of the earth at 1 km intervals with MPEG-2 video, has now become a possibility.

In 1998, the software industry reached a turning point: the decisions made will determine the direction to be taken by software architectures of the future. This trend is accelerated by the convergence of computer, communication and consumer electronics. The once-dominant operating system, such as Windows 3 booted from DOS, will make an exit. Windows NT is now on the verge of addressing the need to support inexpensive computers and a limited range of device support.

Microsoft has begun certain development efforts which will make Windows NT usable as a consumer operating system, thereby making Windows. 136 a more stable platform. A 64-bit architecture, the next paradigm shift in computing, is another new development. To the more than 4 billion bytes of space in a 32-bit address, 4 billion more bytes are being added. Thanks to the memory-mapped file system, programmers will not be required to open, close, read from or write to files any more. The operating system will move the bytes between disk and memory as required to get the data structure from the operating system that contains the data in the file. The new architecture will also allow for the use of integers instead of floating point numbers in many applications, thereby increasing the processing speed and simplifying programming efforts.

User friendiness

The year 1998 also saw the beginning of a shift away from professional intermediaries by associating users directly with their software. As a result, users will be required to learn how to express their problems, set up and adapt computations and carry out tasks such as configuration, upgrade, back-up and recovery. To attain this goal, software system designers have had to redefine user-friendliness.

As a result, software carriers like the Web, Integrated Office Suites, Interactive Environment and Visual Basic, which create their own environment from locally available resources, have become popular because they allow users to create or modify software to correspond to their needs. The setting up of stand-alone processes that can run unmonitored requires an open-ended set of computations - independent processes in mail filters, automatic cheque payment and Daemons, which are sets of software routines and instructions for automating network management tasks.

In another move tò user-friendliness, sparked by the concept of a hyper-linked design of the World Wide Web, the user interface on personal computers has begun to imitate human perception. The Graphic User Interface is inventing software products that organize information graphically in more and more intuitively appealing ways. Continuous speech recognition programmes from International Business Machines (IBM), Dragon Systems and others, have started a process whereby speech recognition will be added to the existing programmes like the speech-enabled version of Lotus Notes.

Databases

The development of Object-Oriented Data-base Management Systems has accelerated to overshadow the traditional Relational Data Base Management (RDBM) software development. Object-Oriented databases allow new data types to be created with traditional attributes found in relational models as well as built-in functions, methods and objects which are convenient for applications requiring video and image content.

However, the growing popularity of data mining (the 'mining' of numerical data in repositories such as spreadsheets and databases) and data warehousing (the gathering of data from legacy mainframe and PC server databases into gigantic centralized databases) has made it possible to keep RDBMS in use. The inter-operability of the Distributed Component Object Model (D-COM) and of Java running on Common Object Request Broker Architecture (CORBA) made databases capable of mixing and matching data in an unprecedented manner. These two trends have brought about a hybrid technology that patches object capabilities on to traditional RDBMS products. Data visualization is a new graphics application which displays in a graphical form the trends that the numbers represent. The evolving Extensible Markup Language (XML) and dynamic Hyper Text Markup Language (HTML) are being integrated to give better graphics on the Web, and new graphics software is +being developed for data mining to bring out anyhidden information. PCs featuring 3-D graphics and exceeding current performance are actively being developed which will increase immersive experience, as if sound and graphics were surrounding the user.

Virtual Reality

Virtual Reality (VR) is now regarded as a natural extension of interactive multimedia. New immersive interfaces like Vision Dome and Immersive Work Bench allow several workers to co-operate and interact in conducting simulation experiments on virtual prototypes. With highspeed networks and the World Wide Web, work may be carried out from almost any geographical location. Architects and furniture wholesalers have already begun using VR on the Web in 3-D by using Virtual Reality Modeling Language (VRML) to give customers a wide selection of simulated prototypes from which to choose.

During 1997 and 1998, there was a rush to create World Wide Web-enabled Software that could be used over the Internet, Intranets and Extranets for exchanging data, with a web site to run programmes, control experiments remotely or publish documents on a network. A significant software-related development has been a shift towards the Web-centred work environment and the electronic distribution of information.

One major deficiency of the Web, namely the limitation of HTML in dealing with mathematics, has been reasonably solved. Instead of the past practice of representing equations as embedded graphics, which proved highly inefficient, an extension of HTML, called Math ML, has been developed.

Many new developments have encouraged the electronic publication of journals , some of which have replaced the paper versions. One of the most significant developments of software applications in 1997 and 1998 saw the rise of the Enterprise Resources Planning (ERP) package, offering a completely new opportunity for organizations to plan their resources around growing customer demand and to offer leading-edge solutions, reduced turnaround time, increased efficiency and improved profit margins. ERP integrates the entire enterprise from suppliers-retailers to customers, and covers departments as functionally independent as finance, production and distribution.

Virtual Communities

In 1997 and 1998, the concept of network-based virtual communities, which will redefine the relationship between companies and customers, gained ground. The emphasis is shifting away from the retailers and is allowing customers to deal directly with wholesalers for the purchase of products and services by capturing and managing information themselves. This is promising to become a beneficial situation for both customers and wholesalers.

Virtual communities will act as agents for their subscribers who will receive adequate, accurate and timely information on products and services; they can purchase at a lower price and with better quality, while this same medium - so supporters claim - meets the social need for communication.

The wholesalers will find the virtual community to be a powerful vehicle for expanding their markets, since the very concept is oriented away from brand images. They will also benefit from the increased propensity of customers to buy, and from reduced marketing costs of customer searching. Wholesalers will also receive a better statistical picture of changing customer tastes and choices and be able to target products to a subset of customers judged more likely to purchase. Above all, the overhead of building retail outlets will be minimized, while an online networked environment will reach a much broader customer base with no geographical limits.

The virtual community requires a technological strategy based on speed and leverage, with the emphasis on modular technology architecture and a focused information infrastructure. The choice of the network platform is between participation in an online service or the Internet. The strength of the Internet lies in its enormous diversity of resources assembled in one networking environment, and the TCP/IP and HTML standards offer more opportunity for growth and innovation than proprietary platforms. Widespread developments of new technologies are taking place to make the Internet the best choice for the virtual community. Thousands of millions of dollars invested in conventional networks, with voice-dominant circuit-switched analog networks, are being threatened by the widespread popularity of the IP-based data networks. The IP packet as the natural medium of exchange was adopted so quickly that the growth of data and voice-over-data traffic increased sharply in 1997 and 1998.

Local Area Networks

In the local area networks, or LANs, switching technology has resulted in Fast Ethernet in the range of 100 Mb/s and Gigabit Ethernet in the range of 1 Gb/s. Asynchronous Transfer Mode (ATM) has proved useful in full backbone networks as well as in Synchronous Optical Networks (SONETs).

According to a worldwide survey conducted by Dell's Oro Group, the market for ATM switches and concentrators increased by 77% from 1996 to 1997, and 60% from 1997 to 1998. ATM is also a leader in the MAN/WAN for inter-building and intra-campus connectivity, and is becoming an important infrastructure for public carrier networks. Such ATM networking is bringing significant synergies to the operation of IP networks, allowing for true integration of multiple traffic types on the same network infrastructure.

Wireless LANs have strengthened only in areas where optical fibre networks with high bandwidth are either absent or deficient. Wireless systems have provided good solutions to the last mile problem in MANs. For this, the Multi-channel, Multi-point Distribution System (MDS) in the two GHz band and as the Local Multi-point Distribution System (LMDS) in the high-frequency band between 26 GHz and 30 GHz have found wide acceptance. With cellular phones, the digitalization process is gaining ground.

Data Transmission

Trends in Europe are towards the growth of Integrated Services Digital Networks (ISDN), which is not the case in North America. The speed and reliability of ISDN at a typical data transmission rate of 128 Kb/s has made it attractive for homes and small businesses. A serious competitor for ISDN is Asymmetric Digital Subscriber Line (ADSL) technology, which allows data to flow downstream towards the subscriber at rates of up to 6 Mb/s. Both are suitable for Internet access.

Satellite Telecommunications

Although INMARSAT-A was first launched in 1991 as an alternative to VSATs by offering high transmission speeds from a miniature ground terminal, the latest version called INMARSAT-B Duplex High Speed Data (HSD) service has now become commercially available in all oceanic regions. It supports highspeed file transfer, store and forward video, video conferencing as well as voice, fax and data transmission. A large number of users including government agencies, international organizations, multinational companies and broadcast service providers have found the services useful.

Many of the above-mentioned development, like ATM and SONET, have led to the creation of networked multimedia systems, which offer several advantages for transmitting still and moving images, graphics, texts and sound; a number of content-rich applications are pushing multimedia communications forward.

Motorola's $3,400 million Iridium venture, with a constellation of 66 satellites and ground links to hand-held phones, was the beginning of a new race among the giants of the satellite business. Competitors such as Loral's 48- satellite Global Star System, the Echostar System and Hughes Electronics Constellation, among others, will probably place ten times the present number 150 commercial satellites into orbit over the next decade. From the present $9,000 million annual revenue from satellite services, the year 2000 is expected to see nearly $30,000 million. Such Low Earth Orbiting (LEO) Satellite systems (they orbit about 1,000 km above the earth) and Medium Earth Orbit (MEO) satellites will bring about a revolution in global voice, paging and fax systems, as well as usher in the next stage of broad-band multi-satellite systems offering fast Internet and video.

Compared to the $30,000 million invested in the cable television industry over the past two decades, the satellite telecommunications industry has invested more than $20,000 million in the past five years and has lined up $60,000 million for the next five.

One of the keys to making satellites pervasive has been the reduction in the cost and size of user terminals by concentrating power more intensely on smaller geographic areas and by reusing precious frequency spectrums many times over. The growth of the Internet and other distributed networks is making star networks less and less effective. Consequently, in 1997 and 1998, commercial satellites with on-board processing, allowing signals to be switched between spot beams in the satellites, began to appear.

The World Wide Web

The World Wide Web is a window open to the tens of millions of pages available online. In addition to being a provider of video services, the Web is a major market driver for broad-band networking. At the beginning of 1997, an estimated 30 million users worldwide used the Web for work, education and recreation at home. With the increase of multimedia applications, Web content is becoming more and more tailored to fast networks. Web browsers have already become universal Graphical User Interfaces (GUIs) for narrow-band services like e-mail, file transfer, transaction processing, Web surfing, and so on. The technology of the Web browser has been extended to broad-band GUIs. The strong signalling requirements for networking systems imposed by Web access saw the beginning of a signalling crisis in 1998, because not all network types could comply with the signalling requirements necessary in broad-band systems. One way of solving this problem was to move from pull mode to push mode data. Push mode allows the servers and networks that provide content to make more efficient use of the available bandwidth and processing time. An important application of push mode data is software updates received from Web Servers. In push mode, the service provider can control content and timing, and it is therefore becoming popular with advertisers.

Internet Telephony

Voice-over-data and IP telephony (VOIP) systems grew exponentially in 1997 and 1998 with a perceptible reduction in telephone tariffs, though at the cost of telephone quality. At present, the IP networks, including the Internet, are not ready for voice-over-data traffic on a very large scale. While waiting for the advent of broadband Internet-II to offer long term solutions, users will continue to experience the effect of overloading on voice quality. IP telephony includes voice-over LANs, Internet, Intranets and Extranets. Both real-time and store-and-forward fax traffic can also be addressed as can unified messaging over the Web.

IP-based Consumer Electronics

Personal computers and digital TVs are converging into one integrated product. Current PCs are constructed with video receiver cards, whereas televisions, with embedded microprocessors required for electronic programme guide (EPG) and digital decoding, have already been built on a pilot scale. Only a small incremental cost is required to add more power and memory to transform a television set into a computer. Services such as Web TV from Microsoft and Intercast are already narrowing the gap between the Web and television. Efforts are under way to establish a consistent link between the Web television so that broadcasters can create a new form of entertainment. High Definition TV (HDTV) is a high-quality digital TV development, delivering data services and multiple channels.

Super-high definition image system (SHD), with a resolution equal to that of a 35-mm film and data capacity four times that of HDTV, has been introduced to make it possible to read stored newspapers even when they are displayed at actual size. This SHD image system may be combined with a Digital Network Library system to provide versatile applications such as a Digital Museum. A seamless video environment can be created by employing ATM-based 150 Mbps HDTV encoding SHD large-screen display technology and tandem HDTV screens with minimal gap between the screens.

In this context, it should be pointed out that data broadcasting standards remain problematic. It may be assumed that Web standards will prevail, but adapting Web standards to a purely broadcasting environment is proving difficult.

Video on demand (VoD) is an emerging service currently under trial. VoD enables consumers to order films, documentaries and educational broadcast/content over a network. As a pull-mode service, no two subscribers are likely to be watching the same film or using the same VCR control such as 'rewind' and 'fast forward'. Separate data flows can therefore be established for each viewer using a bandwidth allocated to a single consumer. With digital com-pressionas one of the enabling technologies for VoD with MPEG, a film of television broadcasting quality can be stored in 3 GB of memory and then played out at 3 Mb/s. A variation, called near video on demand (nVoD), is also at the pilot stage.

Over the past two years, the set-top-box has gained consumer popularity as a supplement to the televison set. The set-top-box is used to provide capacity not present in the TV or VCR by including a slot for 'additional functions', along with a tuner appropriate for the transmission medium. Transmission can be by cable, direct broadcast satellite (DBS), microwave TV, multi-channel, multi-point distribution service (MMDS), cellular TV that uses 28 GHz wireless cable service, or other such devices. Current services made possible by the set-top-box are navigation and interactive programming systems that use on-screen images and cursor-like devices to allow subscribers to select and interact with other services including home shopping, video on demand, electronic games, educational programmes, electronic publishing and telecommunication services like the Internet.

The set-top-box and even television sets have been developed with an embedded network computer (NC). Whereas networked PCs provide each user with local storage and processing with much of the data located within the mainframe, NC goes a step further by distributing data, programmes and computing power across many nodes on the Internet or Intranets. TCP/IP protocol, Inter-programme communication, a mobile code like Java and data representation and retrieval such as HTML and structured query language (SQL) allow for a distributed architecture. NC provides a lower cost alternative to standard PCs for Internet communication.

Multimedia

Multimedia is situated at the crossroads of a large number and variety of technologies and economic sectors. Furthermore, the industry is developing all the time, and available statistics therefore quickly become unreliable and out of date. This problem is compounded by a lack of coherent definitions, which obscures both factual and conceptual analysis. On many points there are differing opinions, and it is not the purpose of this brief overview to support any particular view, but simply to provide the reader with the information needed to understand the ways in which this rapidly expanding sector is developing.

The basic and fairly limited definition of multimedia, is that of 'media in which spatial data (text, image and sound) are merged with temporal data (voice and video), by means of a unifying object - the computer'.

On the basis of this definition, a much broader one with the accent on the transformation of the media could be suggested. In this light, the multimedia revolution is seen to result from the development of the following three types of media:

— *Computers*: thanks to high-level languages such as Hypertalk, Lingo and Java, multimedia producers no longer need to be computer experts to create documents which combine text, sound and image on a compact disk-read only memory (CD-ROM), CD-Interactive (CD-I), Digital Versatile Disk (DVD) or the Internet.

— *Digital video*: television is moving towards interactive television (I-TV) and video on demand, offered by cable distribution networks.

— *Network superhighways* carrying Internet traffic and the information of the future, on which all kinds of interactive services such as electronic mail, voice telephony and videoconferencing, electronic commerce are already flourishing, and soon, perhaps, television on demand.

Multimedia can also be defined in terms of industries. In this context, it can be said to be a result of the convergence of several 'traditional' industries, mainly computer science and communications, and the 'content' industries, such as the audiovisual, publishing, sound recording and media industries. Businesses in these different sectors are merging or forming partnerships and alliances, thus blurring the boundaries between sectors which used to be relatively autonomous.

This multifarious revolution has had a number of political and economic consequences: decompartmentalization of the media industries following the deregulation of the communications industry, convergence of networks, globalization of the cultural industries, and the creation of major multimedia conglomerates which control both content and the vehicles for providing that content.

Hypermedia came into being in the 1980s with the 'Hypertext' of Apple computers, and subsequently spread to all types of data (graphics, fixed images, video sequences, animations, sound) which could be digitized. But it was the 'hyperdocument', closely identified with a given language and material, which became what we now know as 'multimedia', and applied not only to off-line productions such as CD-ROMs or interactive terminals, but also to applications available on networks and on the Internet in particular.

The development of 'hypermedia' was made possible by the following three basic processes: Digitization. In multimedia, the computer's main function is no longer calculation, but management, creation and publishing of vast masses of digitized data - both content and services - in text, graphic, audio or audiovisual form.

The original media through which these data were transmitted were extremely diverse. Today, digitized electronic data is the single medium and a computer is the common processing tool. This creates an entirely new environment where the possibilities for creation and use are endless, and probably as yet largely unexplored. 'Multimediation' of data. It may be appropriate here to establish the difference between audiovisual and multimedia material.

Audiovisual producers work on documents containing data in several formats, for example image, voice/sound, text and graphics. It is not possible to merge all these data, however, because they are organized differently and use different languages. Producers therefore piece the data together in the form of a 'collage', rather than, accurately speaking, merging them. For example, a film with sound or a slide show requires separate editing processes and meticulous synchronization. Hypermedia, on the other hand, digitizes all the data and stores it in memory. It is therefore the computer, with its high-level languages, which controls all the operations involved in production, processing and reading.

Although there is a single basic medium, hypermedia allows a whole range of formats to be used in an integrated manner, from the creation of the product through final use. People who use, consult or work on multimedia products do not do so sequentially, i.e. from start to finish, as when reading a book or watching a film. They move around in this universe of knowledge, guided simply by their intuition, the questions they ask, association of ideas or sensations. They 'navigate' their way around knowledge.

The power to navigate in a non-linear fashion, i.e. by association of ideas, within a relational database, is greatly increased by the ability to act at any given moment. The designers or users of hypermedia products have an ongoing 'dialogue' with the product they are designing/using via their computer. The interactivity of the new systems opens up vast possibilities for human partners who are able to control operations and anticipate results at all times.

The provisional definition of multimedia proposed earlier is bound to change rapidly and spread to all media. The interactive counterparts of the traditional media are flourishing: interactive television, interactive cinema, interactive press, etc. All cultural industries will soon be 'invaded' by multimedia. Furthermore, everyday the Internet makes further inroads into the areas of commerce, business and industry, resulting in the development of an increasing number of multimedia products such as intranets, extranets, electronic commerce, reference databases, and so on.

Multimedia represent one stage in the development of traditional methods for producing, processing, sending and disseminating data. One of the main characteristics of multimedia is its added value in the case of games, reference works, promotional tools, bank and commercial transactions, training and communication.

Multimedia can also be a way of creating innovative concepts. The evolution of supply and demand for these new types of products and services will be closely bound up with technological developments and the adoption of multimedia technologies. Between 1997 and 1998, the introduction of all-digital data turned the multimedia production and distribution landscape upside down.

Two main axes - the functional and the inter-active-relating to this 'added value' can be distinguished. The first is a measure of the increased degree of productivity and efficiency compared to those of traditional methods, and the second is a measure of the level of interactivity, simulation and real-time use.

This classification provides a basis for assessing the value of multimedia and the positioning of the different products and services likely to be offered in the short and long term, as well as establishing the likelihood of their penetrating the market. For example, applications which are high on both the functional and interactive axes, such as recreational learning applications, interactive training, etc., are the most complex and difficult applications to set up.

All players involved in the multimedia industry are affected by the changes taking place. There have been a great many acquisitions and mergers; firms have restructured; new players and production companies are springing up all the time; geographical areas of excellence' are growing and new products are constantly being developed.

The consequences of this constantly-changing market are so great that the usual definitions and data do not adequately reflect the true economics of multimedia. Instead, they are an illustration of 'imperfect' statistical systems inherited from the past, which have difficulty in keeping up with the changes brought about by the transformation of the media and cultural industries. For this reason, it is important to identify methodological signposts and the market trends.

The added value process of today's communications industries is strongly influenced by the impact of multimedia. It may therefore be said to be 'technology-driven'. The market is made up of three main sectors of targeted end-users: individuals and consumers, companies and economic organizations, and institutions.

The central driving force of the model consists of the notions of vehicles (the result of telecommunications and computer technologies) and content (cultural products in the general sense of the word) which correspond to a process that develops horizontally, from one end of the system (upstream) to the other (downstream). Between the two, the idea of integration has been introduced to reflect a sector which acts as a packager, or distribution/ dissemination intermediary, between vehicles (computerized systems and networks) and content (media, new media, and cultural industries).

Multimedia is present in all fields: from the media to the arts, education, consultancy services and museums. However, it is very difficult to pinpoint the extent to which products in these areas can be said to be truly 'multimedia'. Similarly, it is difficult to estimate the economic weight of multimedia in its various forms. In museums, for example, multimedia may account for only one particular aspect of a specific work or exhibition.

The degree of multimedia found in the above-mentioned fields is small but growing, although it is often difficult to determine the percentage of true multimedia activity. For example, there is multimedia content on the Internet, but the Internet as a whole cannot be said to be multimedia, since at least 80% of its content consists of on-line text, i.e. electronic data in text form.

It is very difficult, or even impossible, to determine the exact percentage of true multimedia activity as the concept of interactivity is infinitely elastic, and there is a world of difference between the interactivity of a video recorder and that of a video-game console. Similarly, although there is much talk now of interactive television, very few households actually possess this technology and, as a result, there are as yet no statistics on the subject.

Multimedia products can be developed on various types of media, such as diskette, CD-ROM, CD-I, DVD-ROM, interactive terminals, and 'closed' or on-line networks. However, they tend to be grouped into two broader categories: on-line media and off-line applications. On-line products can be consulted via telephone networks, cable or broadband networks known as 'information superhighways' such as the Internet.

According to Canadian data for 1995, most multimedia applications are still designed for diskette or CD-ROM. The third most common medium (37% of users) for multimedia applications is the interactive terminal, followed by closed and on-line networks. However, mixed applications (part on-line, part off-line) are coming into use: Internet sites twinned with a DVD, for example (the DVD serves as the mass memory and contains the majority of data, while the Internet site makes it possible to update information, and communicate with the network).

However, as on-line multimedia services flourish, the proportion of off-line applications, such as CD-ROMs, should decrease. Some believe that optical discs will eventually disappear as the popularity and capacity of networks increase. Interactive kiosks are another way in which multimedia products can be used by the general public.

For example, Canadian job centres have installed interactive kiosks in public places in order to advertise job vacancies. Similarly, a growing proportion of venues of cultural interest and tourist attractions are equipped with such kiosks to promote their products and services, as are department stores and shopping malls.

Different sources of information on sales of multimedia products and services all show a marked increase in the income generated by this sector since the beginning of the 1990s, and this increase is set to continue over the next ten years. The international study by Frost and Sullivan - World Multimedia Application Market - points to a significant increase in this sector.

The overall growth in the market is reflected both in the demand for products on optical media and in the use of on-line services. The demand for multimedia products is mainly concentrated in North America, where in 1994 sales of applications totalled approximately $4,000 million

- nearly 50% of world sales. However, the share of international revenue generated by the American market will decrease over time to the advantage of other geographical regions, in particular the Pacific.

Demand for multimedia products and services is currently measured in terms of the use of optical discs, since this is the most common support medium used for multimedia products and services. Direct, on-line access to these services is, in most cases, still at the development stage.

Worldwide sales of CD-ROMs (databases, images, sound and multimedia) totalled 8 million units in 1993, 16.5 million in 1994 and 53.9 million in 1995. The number of CD-ROMs available on the market also showed a staggering increase of 800% between 1990 and 1995, yielding an average annual growth rate of 51%. It should be said that multimedia productions in 1995 accounted for only 25% of the total number of CD-ROMs in circulation (75% of all CD-ROMs presumably contained other data). The United States is the main geographical market for multimedia applications. In 1994, 55% of all optical disk drives were used in the United States, compared to 19% in Japan, 14% in Europe and 12% in the rest of the world. The number of these drives - a variable which is directly related to the size of the market - has grown at a rate of 56% per year since 1992 in the United States.

The enthusiasm for multimedia applications has also led to a significant rise in demand for on-line services, especially for data communications networks and direct-access databases. The Internet is the main data communications network on a world scale, and links some 100,000 networks in more than two hundred countries. The explosion of this network has created a huge market of users of multimedia products. Unfortunately there are no reliable data on the subject.

It is very difficult to compare differences and similarities between different countries regarding the use of multimedia products with any accuracy owing to the lack of reliable data and clear definitions at present. The following are very difficult to classify, for example: video games for children, recreational applications, erotic productions, tourism CD-ROMs, PlayStation CDs, Nintendo cassettes, vocational training CDs and educational CDs.

Despite these difficulties, several major trends can be distinguished - at least for the time being - in the world market of multimedia products for the following types of applications: computer games; dictionaries, encyclopaedias, knowledge databases, technical literature, etc.; arts and culture; educational and training software; and professional applications.

In the United States, according to the study carried out by the Information Workstation Group in 1993, most of the revenue from the multimedia sector came from professional and business applications. Products for the general public in the leisure and reference sector (dictionaries, encyclopaedias, information, etc.) account for 34% of the market, while educational products make up 12% of sales.

At first sight, these results may appear dubious, since electronic games, which are reputed to be a strong point in the United States, come second in the list of the most widely used consumer CD-ROMs. If this is the case, one can only assume that PlayStation, Saturn and Nintendo applications were not taken into account in this study! In France, sales of CD-ROM products on the market fall into the categories of games, art, literature and cinema productions, and applications for children and professionals. Games account for only 49% of sales, five points down on the previous year. Most new products on the market fall into the 'education' category, and CD-ROM sales in this category - which have been boosted by the arrival of electronic encyclopaedias and dictionaries - have accordingly tripled in one year, from 7% in 1996 to 22% at the end of 1997, making this the highest-growth sector of all. The third-ranking sector, 'Art and culture', accounts for only 15% of sales of CD-ROMs, despite a 38% increase in the number of CD-ROMs issued. The category 'Practical information and tourism' has seen an increase similar to that in educational applications: 12% of sales in 1997, compared to only 7% in 1996.

According to a study by Industrie Canada. Canadian multimedia production seems geared primarily to the business, government and education sectors. However, given that most applications found on the market originated in the United States, these data do not give an accurate picture of the use of multimedia products and services.

Retail trade is also making a considerable breakthrough, but companies specializing in catalogue sales have realized that the operation will be long and difficult. These firms make only a small fraction of their catalogue available on line, since creating an interesting and attractive on-line catalogue is still a difficult and time-consuming task. CDs and books sell well on the Internet. CD sales are set to reach $20 million, with profits in the region of $200,000, according to The Red

Herring. However, MCI, a telephone company, has just closed its 1-8 0 0-M u s i c-Now site, after spending $40 million and selling only 400 CDs. Nevertheless, the research firm Jupiter predicts that in the year 2000, $ 1 8 6 million - 2% of total revenue - will be generated in this way in this sector. Two major American sites,. Barnes & Noble and Borders, are competing with the British Bookshop site. However, more optimistic predictions put the figure for revenue generated via on-line networks in the year 2000 at 8%, not 2%, citing the unprecedented success of the Amazon Web site.

Automobiles are also sold via networks on sites such as Autobuytel, which was set up by Peter Ellis in California. For a monthly fee of between $250 and $1,000, 1,400 people posted car-sale advertisements on the site, generating revenue of $6.5 million for the company. Out of 15 million cars sold in the United States, 2 million vehicles were bought after just one visit to the sales room, which indicates that purchasers know exactly what they want.

Chrysler sold 1.5% of its cars through its Internet address, and believes it can increase this figure to 25%. It costs customers only $25 to buy a car through a Web site. Advertising and marketing are well represented on the Internet, as each day thousands of corporate sites, featuring multimedia to varying degrees, are created. However, this does not mean that all these marketing operations are effective.

The cost of a multimedia application varies enormously according to the type of product. Two main factors influence the total costs and how these costs are broken down: the quality of the finished product (high- or low-quality item), the type of product and the market sector for which it was designed (consumer product, educational product, or corporate product), and lastly, the scale of the finished product. To give an idea, it may be said that production costs vary between $135,000 and $4 million. Of these figures, 60% represents the cost of the production itself, with the rest divided between pre-production, post-production and miscellaneous costs.

Some dictionaries and encyclopaedias cost from $1 million to $4 million to produce, if the years of research necessary for finalizing the content are taken into account. Apart from the overall costs, how costs are broken down according to different components varies according to the type of product. For example, a 'game'-type application requires much more programming than an educational application. Analysing the distribution of CD-ROMs is often difficult. It is not always clear whether they should be classed as computer products, literary or artistic works, or video games.

In the United States, 40%-45% of all CD-ROMs are 'bundled' - in other words offered free with the purchase of multimedia equipment or specialized journals. When CD-ROMs are sold individually, most are distributed through specialist computer distributors. In France, sales from hypermarkets are not increasing as much as they are through other market channels. Hypermarkets now account for only 34% of all software sold, compared to 40% in 1996. Most sales are now made in specialized computer hyper-markets, which sold 39% of software in 1997, compared to 36% in 1996. Two other categories of distributor have seen their market shares rise. These are games and CD specialists, which now sell some 11% of leisure software, compared to 9% in 1997, and toy specialists, with 5% of sales, compared to 3% the previous year.

The Internet

Information is a vast category, covering stock-market transactions, financial information, daily news services such as Reuters, and databases such as Nexis and Lexis. According to Simba Information, this market is worth $11,000 million, but at present not all these services can be accessed via the Internet - far from it! For example, in the field of financial services, the research company Forrester estimates that the volume of financial transactions taking place on-line this year will be worth $111,000 million, and that this figure will have reached $474,000 million by the year 2000. Swarb, a San Francisco stockbroking firm, estimates that one sixth of its business last year was done on line, accounting for a total of 700,000 transactions. A further thirty broking firms offer similar services.

There are hundreds of journals and magazines on the Internet, and several major newspapers already have electronic versions, whether these are partial or total, adapted or identical to the paper version. Some operations were amazingly successful, such as Hot Wired (the Web site of the American journal Wired), but other magazines closed when the electronic version proved stronger than the paper version. It should be added that not all on-line information is of a multimedia nature; only a very small proportion does in fact combine text, image and video sequences in an interactive language.

Erotic content sells well when the confidentiality of transactions is ensured. The research firm Forrester states that 10% of sales via the Internet are of a sexual nature, whether in the form of books, video-clips, photographs, on-line interviews, or other items. These sales amount to $52 million, and there are thousands of sites on the

Internet. The Seattle-based Internet Entertainment Group has 50,000 subscribers paying for its on-line service, the same as the number of subscribers to the Wall Street Journal! Travel is another sector which is becoming increasingly important on the Internet.

Most airline companies have a Web site through which they sell seats directly, often offering a discount of 5%, the equivalent of the travel agent's commission (as is the case, for example, with Northwest and Continental airlines). However, Expedia, the leader in its category, has total sales of nearly $1 million, with Internet sales accounting for at most 1% of its total revenue. According to Forrester, again, sales in this sector are set to increase by 50% over the next three years.

In the world, most people who encounter the Internet consider it to be a vibrant medium of exchange that supports a wide variety of uses, most of them commercial. Many also know that, having been created with support from the United States Government, Defence Advanced Research Project Agency (DARPA) initially, and later the National Science Foundation (NSF), the Department of Education (DOE) and other agencies and departments, the Internet has its roots in the research and development community.

In recent years, the private sector has made extensive investments in building Internet capabilities, and its recent growth has been almost entirely fuelled by such private sector initiatives. However, as recently as a decade ago, the Internet was still the private enclave of the research and education community. At that time, few in the telecommunications business believed that the private sector would come to play such a critical role in leading its continued development and that the Internet would come to play such a central role in the United States (and indeed the world's) economy in the short span of ten years.

The Internet is a collection of networks around the world that inter-operate seamlessly via an open architecture and its associated protocols. The first three networks in the Internet were the Advanced Research Project Agency Network (ARPANET), packet radio network, and packet satellite network, all sponsored by DARPA several decades ago.

Each of these three networks was individually designed and implemented, but most importantly, the Internet architecture was created to be independent of the detailed design or implementation of any of its constituent networks.

As a result, the technology for networking could evolve and change, and the latest technology could be integrated with the prior technology simply by adding new networks. The success of the Internet was therefore heavily dependent on the underlying computer communications technology that had been pioneered in the ARPANET.

The basic notions of packet switching were already well known by the late 1960s and had been successfully demonstrated in the ARPANET project by the early 1970s. In addition, the notion of layered host protocols, also demonstrated in the ARPANET project, allowed for building new applications and services on top of existing ones, and has been carried forward to the present as a basic paradigm for protocol implementation.

To get to the Internet architecture was not a completely straightforward path, however, from the early network developments. In fact, the original implementation of the packet satellite network equipment assumed it would be integrated into upper memory of an ARPANET IMP (Interface Message Processors), and not be a separate, externally accessible network.

This was perhaps the first of many cases where the network management required close co-ordination with network architecture and raised the basic issue of overall governance of the 'network of networks'. As is now known, there is no single entity responsible for the overall performance of the Internet, as there is no entity responsible for the performance of the world economy.

Some perceive this as a fatal weakness; others, as a principal strength. Whatever their views, all the participants have a fundamental interest in the success of the system and will generally do their part to contribute to it, while recognizing that they may need to work together on certain problems and issues that cannot be resolved in isolation. Networking development over the past four decades may generally be categorized as follows:

— The period of the 1960s, in which basic ideas emerged for computer networking, particularly those of packet switching and the possibilities for sharing resources over computer networks.

— The period of the 1970s, when packet switching technology was developed and demonstrated in several experimental and commercial networks, beginning with the ARPANET at speeds of 50 Kbps. This was mainly a period of technological development, including the development of local area networks like the Ethernet and small computers such as the Xerox Alto for individual users that presaged the personal computer as we now know it.

— In the 1980s, widespread deployment and commercialization of the technology began. Networking was extended to the entire research and higher-education communities. Industry took to manufacturing and selling personal computers and workstations, local-area networks, and related software. Transmission Control Protocol/ Internet Protocol (TCP/IP) became the standard protocol for computer communications. The National Science Foundation Network (NSFNET) replaced the ARPANET as the backbone of the Internet at speeds of 1.5 Mbps. By the late 1980s, there were thousands of networks and tens of thousands of hosts on the then emerging Internet. Most of these were local and regional networks that had been formed during the decade.

— The 1990s has been the decade of commercialization of the Internet. Beginning with the first experiments to link commercial e-mail. Evolution of the Internet 159 systems to the government-supported (and, at the time, still-dominant) portion of the Internet, the desirability of allowing commercial interactions on the NSFNET grew. The ARPANET was decommissioned. The Boucher Bill, passed by United States House of Representatives in early 1993, opened up the National Science Foundation Network (NSFNET) to commercial use.

A few years later, sufficient private sector networking capability was deemed to exist, and US Federal government support for the NSFNET ceased. Although the Internet was growing at 100% per year prior to 1993, the introduction of the Mosaic browser for the World Wide Web caused usage of the Internet to accelerate dramatically. It is now widely assumed that, by the end of this decade, approximately 100 million users will have access to the Internet. A decade later the number might easily be a factor of ten larger, representing perhaps 10% of the world's population.

While the decision by the United States Government to privatize key parts of the Internet, such as the Domain Name System (DNS), became embroiled in debate across many continents, this is not a new phenomenon. Indeed, the move to privatization has been taking place steadily over many decades.

In the late 1970s, DARPA began to involve the research community in the decision-making process for A R PANET standards, and by the mid-1980s, this basic responsibility had been assumed by the research community. As part of its strategy from the beginning, NSF encouraged and, in several cases, funded the development of local and regional research networks by the private sector.

With support for the Internet Engineering Task Force (IETF) and the Internet Assigned Numbers Authority, NSF empowered these groups to take responsibility for leading the effort to establish standards. In working with the Internet Society and various diverse groups from many quarters, it recognized the role that private-sector bodies had to play in the overall organization and governance of the Internet. At this point, with respect to the evolution of the Internet, the essential function of the United States Government, in co-operation with other governments, should be:

— to ensure that a fair process is set up for the evolution of the Internet at the local, national, regional and global level;

— to provide supervisory capability in the event that private-sector efforts fail to ensure fairness or guarantee the effective working of the Internet;

— to remove any bottlenecks, barriers and other obstacles to progress;

— to support advanced research, as appropriate; and

— to address policy issues concerning the Internet, and to encourage or otherwise stimulate progress in the Internet towards the general well being of society.

With the possible exception of the last two, these functions can be quite difficult for governments to carry out effectively. The notion of fairness is likely to be elusive among competing parties, and, left to their own devices, private sector organizations will be more inclined to tilt the process in their own favour whenever possible.

The private sector may provide supervisory functions, but these too must be watched closely, if only in the public interest. Finally, it may be difficult to identify many of the barriers and bottlenecks, let alone to find effective ways to overcome them. It is important that the harbingers of change not be hindered by established ways of doing business. Governments cannot effectively solve these problems unilaterally, but they can and should draw upon input from the private sector. Research is the key to unlocking new capabilities. While industry has the incentive to carry out short-term research, often in the process of product development, with few exceptions, it will not invest for the long-term.

Since the break-up of the Bell System in 1984, the amount of long-term industrial research has remained low. Only states seem able to make the commitment to long-term research funding. The US President's Information Technology Advisory Committee (PITAC) recently recommended that funding for long-term information technology research be significantly increased. This advice is likely to be acted upon positively in the US Congress, although the exact amount of the increase over time will not be known for some time.

At a time when the role of government appears to be diminishing, the issue of Internet governance is also being discussed with some fervour. The notion of a single organization or party being responsible for the overall operation of the Internet seems as unusual as that of a similar body for governance of the world's economy. Each network operator will be subject to one or more governmental regimes and legal systems, and standards that enable interoperability must be maintained and allowed to evolve. This requires collaboration and interchange.

While groups such as the Internet Society and IETF, and more recently the World Wide Web Consortium (W3C) and the Internet Corporation for Assigned Names and Numbers (ICANN) represent efforts among many interested parties to work together, the first steps toward collaboration among the Internet Service Providers were taken during the past decade.

Specific examples are the formation of the Commercial Internet Exchange (CIX) in the late 1980s to facilitate the exchange of traffic among commercial internet service providers, and more recently the formation of the Internet Operators Group known as IOPS.ORG to work on problems and issues concerning performance of the Internet. The formation of ICANN to co-ordinate issues of naming and addressing is merely the most recent development for keeping watch over a portion of the Internet governance problem in a private-sector organization.

In the span of three decades, the speed of network lines has increased from 50 Kb/s to 10 Gb/s. Today, the typical user can access the Internet by dial-up connections at 56 Kb/s or with special local access provisions such as Integrated Services Digital Networks (ISDN) at 128 Kb/s, Cable modems at 10 Mb/s (shared with other cable users on his part of the system), or via various levels of Digital Subscriber Lines (DSL) from the telephone companies at dedicated speeds up to about 6 Mb/s.

The cost of such local connections in the United States ranges from about several dozen dollars per month up to a few hundred, for the most advanced DSL services. At these access speeds, the long-haul portion of the Internet typically costs from a few dozen dollars to a few thousand dollars per month. Yet very few users, if any, have access to the gigabit-per-second throughput capabilities available from some carriers.

There are simply no provisions to supply them to individual users unless they spend considerable sums to commission such services to be provided on an individual case basis. So gigabit speeds are economically impractical for most users at present. For businesses, where the investments can be shared among many users and considered as a business expense, the situation is more manageable, but there is little incentive to make these investments unless the traffic or the applications demand it. If inexpensive local access with consumption-based pricing of long-haul services can be provided, then high-speed capabilities may become affordable for businesses.

Computer and software companies will then have an incentive to produce the needed hardware and software for gigabit applications. The rapid growth of paging, cellular telephony and other wireless applications (including wireless Local Area Networks, or LANs, and Internet access) have caused the prices for wireless devices to drop almost to the level of commodities.

Palm-sized devices with computing capabilities approaching those of full desktop PCs (but with limited display, storage and battery life) have recently emerged and will eventually dominate the market. It is not unlikely that most of these devices will have wireless connections and still remain commodity priced. The ability to stay connected, if one chooses, wherever one goes, is likely to be the norm.

However, small size will ultimately dictate the refinement of speech input technology as a means of controlling computer interactions. Innovative means of display are likely to emerge, as are methods for pointing and selecting within these new contexts. Wireless access at speeds up to 1.5 Mb/s in the next decade seems destined for those who can afford the high cost, but much higher-speed wireless access in the local environment is also possible.

Economics, among other things, will determine if it is practical to provide this capability using wireless technology in place of fibre or to replace copper. Finally, satellite access will continue to be attractive for certain applications, including access into the fixed telecommunications plant at nearby points, or for worldwide communications that do not depend upon the terrestrial communications plant at all.

This field, which was once considered by its inventors as overkill, since it could designate several trillion machines or end devices, is now close to saturation from the widespread proliferation of personal computers. Efforts to accommodate this growth have focused around the development and deployment of IPv6, a 128-bit version of the protocol that augments the original version in several important ways. Although it may seem hard to believe now, we may ultimately find that even such huge numbers as 10 40, are not large enough. This size will enable every device known to have a network address.

With ubiquitous chip-sized computation available for pennies or less, every refrigerator, toaster, oven, furnace, light switch and doorknob can, in principle, be monitored and/or controlled by the authorized parties on the Internet. Proliferation of Digital Information. E-mail has been a fixture on the network since the earliest days of the ARPAN ET, as have computer files and the ability to move them between machines on the network.

The World Wide Web has greatly simplified the mechanics of specifying files as a single string (known as a Uniform Resource Locator, or URL) consisting of the machine name followed by the file name.

Furthermore, the Web design took some of the best features of Standard General Markup Language (SGML), a graphics markup language pioneered by the publishing community, and produced a simplified version called

HTML that was easier to learn. Files written in HTML could be more easily manipulated by computer for presentation on many screens than could files formatted in many different, perhaps even arbitrary ways.

Many users connect to the Internet simply to send and receive e-mail and to access the Web. These two functions are a first important step in making digital information available on the Internet. Recent efforts to create repositories of digital objects that can persist over long periods of time and that can be accessed with precision through sophisticated search mechanisms are almost within reach. These systems, part of an open-architecture approach known generally as 'digital object infrastructure', have the ability to encompass the Web as well as most other information systems.

The future rarely plays out the way we imagine it will, and in the full knowledge that any such predictions are likely to be disproved by practice, the following possibilities may nonetheless be proposed. E-commerce will continue to flourish, with a move away from prepackaged buying options prepared by sellers, to more opportunities for customization and other user-defined products and services.

Intermediate organizations on the Internet will find better ways to match the needs of potential customers and suppliers of goods and services. Better means for locating all kinds of items will be developed, including the ability to locate individuals (primarily those who wish to be found, but possibly some who do not), to locate sources of goods of all kinds including new and used components, and even to trace the history and performance of selected goods and services. Building worldwide markets is largely a nontechnical problem, but technology can greatly assist in this domain. The organization of marketing forces on the Internet is still in its infancy and will probably only increase in sophistication over time.

Collaboration is one of the largely untapped gold mines on the Internet. The applications in which groups or individuals at different locations, and even at different times, work together on missions of common purpose, are potentially enormous, and difficult to carry out effectively via other means. From applications such as IP video and tele-conferencing, which have early prototypes on the low bandwidth of today's Internet, to joint manufacturing design and development, to strategic planning by teams of experts, the field of possibilities is large. Furthermore, applications that involve or even stimulate the development of information as malleable content, to be further worked on by others, while respecting the rights of the original creators, could open up new modes of creativity.

Finally, the potential for the use of sensors, activators and control mechanisms of all kinds on the Internet has remained largely unexplored. Improvements in weather prediction resulted directly from the use of global satellite monitoring systems. It is possible to imagine weather instrumentation deployed on virtually every building, vehicle and individual which is able to report local conditions.

The utility of a three-dimensional fine-grained grid of such weather information, combined with mathematical prediction models could improve our long-range prediction abilities by days, or even weeks. The ability to use the Internet for facilities and operations of all kinds could become routine. The remote operation of manufacturing plants is one example; the possibility of collaborative telemedicine is another.

ICT and Standards-based Instruction

The effective education requires monitoring students' academic progress and using this information to design appropriate instruction. Planning, instruction, and assessment should be closely interconnected and cyclical. Standards-based instruction and assessment, as the word standard implies, means consistency in expectations for student achievement and curriculum coverage and consistency in the standards by which students are evaluated. This requires that standards be clear, specific, and uniform–not fluctuating depending upon which teacher a student gets, what week of the school year it is, or what grade, course, or school s/he happens to be in. Teaching toward clear and consistent standards, assessment of student performance to monitor progress, and utilizing assessment information for instructional planning–these are the elements as 'standards-based instruction and assessment' (SBIA). SBIA is an ideal–a set of principles to strive for. There are many obstacles to realising the ideals of SBIA in schools, but progress has occurred both because of education reform initiatives and developments in information technology in education: namely state standards-based reform policies and web-based systems for reporting standards and assessment results. After elaborating more on SBIA, this paper explains and provides examples of how progress is occurring at the state, district, and school levels. At the same time, there is still far to go and obstacles to overcome before more fully realized versions of SBIA operate effectively at the classroom level.

Ideally, teachers teach toward a clear set of instructional objectives. This statement does not imply a mechanistic pursuit of minutely specified behavioral objectives. While educators disagree on the specifics of good objectives-based instruction, there is virtually universal agreement with the principle that good teachers have a very clear understanding of the instructional outcomes they seek. They are clear on what they want their students to know and be able to do at the culmination of instruction. Good lessons and units have clear and specific academic aims. Effective instructional planning entails thoughtful design and sequencing of lessons and units. Assessment is integral to effective instruction. Good teachers assess the outcomes of their instruction frequently by questioning students and with more formal assessments of student learning, and they use the assessment information in the design of subsequent instruction.

On a moment to moment basis, in the context of instruction, good teachers use a variety of questioning techniques to assess student comprehension and developing proficiencies. Over the longer term, from lesson to lesson, unit to unit, and marking period to marking period, good teachers systematically collect and manage assessment data on their students. Good teachers also evaluate their impact on students over the course of the year, by examining individual and aggregate growth of their students based on appropriate local and norm-referenced and criterion-referenced assessments. Appropriate assessment data include scores on tests, quizzes, and other diagnostic and standardized assessments, as well as grades and other forms of student information useful for instruction. When assessments reveal students are not achieving desired learning outcomes, instruction is revised accordingly. Planning, instruction, and assessment should constitute an ongoing, integrated cycle. Standards-based instruction and assessment requires that teachers teaching at the same grade, whether in different classrooms or schools, be guided by the same content and performance standards. As asserted earlier, this is an ideal, a set of principles to strive for.

Ideally, expectations for student achievement and standards of curriculum content should not be dependent upon what classroom or school a student happens to be in. The planning and delivery of instruction should be guided by and aim toward clearly specified standards. Whether standards prescribe how well students should be able to read or write by certain grade levels, what topics they should cover in particular courses, or what competencies they should demonstrate at graduation, in principle the standard is the same for all students–that is what 'standard' means. The antithesis of standards-based instruction is each teacher independently deciding what will be covered in his/her classroom and the level of achievement expected of the students. Without standards, expectations for student knowledge and achievement and instructional goals are necessarily based on the idiosyncratic preferences of individual teachers. Fully realized at an organizational level, standards-based instruction and assessment (SBIA) requires that the planning, instruction, and assessment cycle be vertically integrated among the school's different levels: student, classrooms, supra-classroom groups, whole school. Standards of achievement should be clearly understood and operate school-wide, with adequate data to monitor performance and processes at organizational and sub-organizational levels.

The model assumes that teachers have a common vocabulary to plan instruction and reflect on practice; plan instruction from a shared understanding of content and achievement standards; evaluate students based on principles and expectations that are consistent across students, groups of students, and periods of time; and participate in instructional management, such as monitoring the effectiveness of instructional programs and identifying instructional and resource allocation priorities for short and long-term planning. Research shows that schools vary widely in their ability to achieve SBIA at an organizational level–with leadership being a critical variable–and that schools that are able to implement effectively principles of SBIA are likely to be better schools.

Planning, instruction, and assessment occur as a cycle to some degree in all classrooms and schools—but to what degree is this process standards-based, informed by assessment data, and integrated at the organizational level? That is, to what degree does it conform to the principles of SBIA? The standards-based reform movement has occurred in large part because many people believe there has been, and perhaps continues to be, a significant gap between instruction in practice and the principles of SBIA. Building in the mid-80s and continuing throughout the 90s, the education standards movement resulted in widespread adoption in almost all states of written standards of content and performance and standards-based testing programs to measure student achievement and school performance. Before turning to some of the accomplishments of standards-based reform in education, let us examine some of the conditions that lead to it. Certainly one of the most significant factors has been the glaring disparities in achievement and presumably academic standards among schools, especially between schools serving lower-income and/or minority populations and schools with more middle-income, non-minority populations.

One notable study with evidence of disparities in standards among schools was reported by the US Department of Education's Office for Educational Research and Improvement. This study found students in low-income schools getting 'mostly As' in reading and math, while students matched on reading and mathematics ability but enrolled in schools with low percentages of kids in poverty were getting 'mostly Cs.' The obvious implication is that reading and mathematics ability levels sufficient to get high grades in lower-income schools, would likely produce only 'Cs' in schools with more higher-income children. Other studies have examined more directly variation in teacher expectations and instructional practices among schools and classrooms. A review of observational research on reading instruction found 'substantial variation across teachers' on such variables as academic focus, classroom management problems, and time-on-task in reading, with predictable relationships with reading achievement. Likewise, a national survey of reading practices found 'considerable variation' among teachers in reported teaching philosophies, learning goals, and instructional practices.

A study of a large sample of teacher-made tests and quizzes from middle school general mathematics courses found teachers' tests varying widely in their level of alignment with the standards published by the National Council of Teachers of Mathematics. Some teachers' tests were composed of more than two-thirds 'single-step/single-solution' computation problems, while for other teachers the percentage was as low as one-third, with the majority of their test questions involving higher levels of mathematical reasoning and problem solving. Teachers varied even more in the extent to which test questions involved contextualized problems, mathematical representations, and written explanations of mathematical reasoning. Teachers ranged greatly in their reliance on multiple-choice formats for their tests from a low of 3% to a high of 42% of tests used in their courses.

The percent of 'low-level' items (answers can be computed in one or two steps) among tests ranged from 55%–90%. The data clearly suggest that teachers' views of what constitutes adequate achievement and their instructional and assessment practices vary widely. As the above studies indicate, the particular teacher to which a student is assigned matters a lot. A growing body of research indicates that differential teacher effectiveness is a strong determinant of differences in student learning, far outweighing the effects of differences in class size and heterogeneity. The teacher to which a student gets assigned to a large degree determines the content s/she will cover, the pedagogy s/he will experience, and the academic standards s/he will be held to. In the absence of clear and consistent standards and standards-based assessment within the school, it stands to reason that there is likely to be more idiosyncratic—standards-free and data-free–instructional planning and assessment, contributing to disparities in achievement expectations and the quality of instruction.

SBIA should be able to reduce the number of students held to substandard academic expectations, subjected to poorly planned and sequenced instruction, and socially promoted through the grades with inadequate skills and undiscovered learning deficiencies. Another factor fostering support for standards-based education reform policies has been the perception of deficient instructional management at the school and district level, perceived in part to be a product of the absence of agreed-upon standards and measurement of results, and limited accountability for results.

Lacking clear standards and good assessment data, the concern is that too many teachers and administrators fall prey to easy, but unexamined, assumptions that standards are high, teachers are teaching effectively, and students are achieving at acceptable levels. If a school has neither clear grade level achievement standards nor standards-based assessments of achievement, it is hard to know whether instruction is effective. It also creates conditions in which ineffective teachers can be buffered from accountability or pressures to improve, while exemplary teachers go unrecognized, with the outcomes of their efforts remaining invisible within the organization. Substandard instruction and learning outcomes are not easily changed if they are not easily identified. Without benchmarks against which to gauge performance and data to support analysis of practice, many schools are rudderless and unable to do much about it. Whether standards-based reforms can fully resolve these problems remains unclear, and is probably unlikely. There is little research specifically on this question, but findings of studies which can speak to this question support that the absence of clear standards and instructional planning information is an obstacle to school effectiveness.

A study comparing successful and unsuccessful schools implementing school-based management found that the successful managers of reform had 'access to a wide variety of information on student, staff, and school performance, and used the information to guide decision making, to provide feedback to school constituents, and to enhance organizational learning'. Other studies emphasize the costs deficient information and bad management: A large study of a systemwide school-based management initiative in Chicago delegating more authority and management responsibility to schools found that most schools did not improve, and a very large proportion, as much as one-third, actually got worse with planning and decision-making in schools crippled by conflict, inadequate information, and poor decision-making. The efficacy of standards-based reform is still more assumed than documented, but there is hope that the gap between SBIA and practice in schools may be lessened by state laws implementing clearer and more ambitious standards, improved assessments of achievement, and stronger accountability sanctions.

Few would dispute that the standards-based reform movement has far to go. But at the same time we must not underestimate the scope of the challenge or overlook progress. The United States' education system is enormously decentralized and has been characterized by leading scholars as fragmented in its governance, loosely-coupled in its organizational structure, and suffused with cultural traditions making management practice and instructional methods highly resistant to change. Faced with these conditions, it will be neither quick nor easy to engender principles of SBIA in schools. Still, standards-based reform has produced some noteworthy systemwide changes.

Twenty years ago few states had educational goal statements specific enough to provide instructional guidance. Now virtually all states have extensive sets of written standards for curriculum content and student achievement referred to as content and performance standards. Content standards prescribe topics that must be covered and performance standards prescribe skills and abilities and specific expectations by certain grades. As states have rewritten and revised these standards over time, the progression has been inexorably one way: states have made content and performance standards more comprehensive and more specific and strengthened their statutory authority. Over that past several decades state-prescribed education goals have become more comprehensive and specific. Content and performance standards have been prescribed at increasing numbers of grades in the K-12 sequence, in increasing numbers of subjects, and with broader scope of coverage at each grade level.

Educational goals, then, have been made clearer, more specific, and more uniform throughout state education systems. In fact, research indicates goals have become more uniform among states within the country. A major component of standards-led education reform has been the production of influential national curriculum. As state curriculum committees across the country worked on revising and upgrading their own documents and standards they often looked to the national curriculum details for guidance while sharing information through networking, conferences, and the like—activities which many observers believe have lead to greater uniformity of standards among states.

The amount of student achievement testing has increased steadily over the years, but more significant for the goals of SBIA, the sophistication of performance measurement has improved. During the 80s statewide testing programs expanded in scope, with testing expanding to cover more grade levels and more subjects. The 90s brought about four important changes.

— There was growing recognition of the limitations of exclusive reliance on norm-referenced comparisons. State testing programs became more criterion-referenced, with scores of students and school mean scores reported in relation to fixed benchmarks derived from published content and performance standards. In addition to reporting, we are at the 55th percentile, a school would our average score is 3.2 on the 5 point scale, where 3.0 is the threshold described as 'at standard'."

— Exclusive reliance on multiple choice formats gave way to mixed formats, tests with both multiple choice items and constructed response items. This in theory makes the tests more valid for measuring problem solving and knowledge integration. Many more states also started using writing tests in which students produce short essays graded by readers.

— States moved toward more analytical measures of school performance reporting. Educators and researchers have long understood that a school's test scores are a function not just of the quality and effectiveness of its staff and programs, but also of the socioeconomic backgrounds of its students. Therefore, comparing schools on 'raw' descriptive statistics, such as the mean of their students' scores on a particular test, is not particularly useful. High scoring schools almost always have low percentages of low-income students; vice versa for the low performing schools. By the late 80s many states began using more analytical measures of school performance. One approach is to adjust for student socioeconomic background and other characteristics considered exogenous to the school, so schools' scores would be compared only to other demographically similar schools. Another approach (not mutually exclusive with demographic adjustments) is to report and evaluate schools' scores on the basis of achievement gains (or losses) over time. Within these broad analytical reporting strategies there are a variety of more specific statistical methods. The main point, though, is over that last fifteen years state education agencies shifted toward the reporting of measures of school performance that are significantly more advanced than mere details of "raw" descriptive statistics.

— School performance measurement has increasingly included information beyond test scores. Other measures of performance have also been added to states' systems for evaluating schools. These include graduation rates, percentages of students taking the SAT, and enrollments in college prep courses.

Educational standards and assessment results can aid decision-making and influence practice only if people know the standards and can access the assessment results. One obstacle to standards-based reform has been that teachers sometimes do not know much in detail about new standards documents; teachers have also confronted difficulties in accessing assessment results. The Internet, local computer networking, and electronic data interchange are overcoming some of these obstacles to access and understanding and therefore increasing the number of teachers and principals using information on standards and results for instruction and instructional management. Prior to the advent of the Internet and computer networking for electronic data interchange, information about goals and performance was distributed exclusively in paper details.

Curriculum guides were printed and bound by state education agencies and then distributed to school district office personnel by mail or at conferences of district curriculum coordinators; district personnel in turn had the responsibility of distributing these documents to schools. It was generally expected that at least one copy would be available in schools' administrative offices and hoped that each teacher would have his/her own set, but this often depended upon the administrators' predilections and photo-copying resources. The same general approach operated with respect of school and school district performance on state tests, although unlike curriculum documents, test data (typically in the form of magnetic tape) would eventually also be sent to school districts. Paper-based, manual distribution of information still occurs–however, there is a parallel process today of electronic information exchange. Virtually all school and district level decision-makers now have access to electronic information. Over 95% of schools have computers connected to the Internet and local area networks.

The infrastructure is in place, then, to profoundly improve access to decision-support information about educational goals, standards, and performance. Throughout the nation, states and districts are using this IT infrastructure to do just that. The typical web-based EDI concerning educational standards and school performance. Information on state content and performance standards is accessed typically through a four step process of web navigation:

(1) the state education agency website;

(2) the office responsible for curriculum/instruction;

(3) the links to 'standards;'

(4) the links to particular content areas and grade levels.

Increasingly, standards documents are displayed in portable document format, but are also in rich text and ascii text formats. This maximizes their accessibility.

The information moves electronically instead of in cartons in trucks, and can be revised without incurring large re-distribution costs. (This is not to say frequent revision is a good idea–far from it.) More important from the perspective of SBIA, is that users always have access to the information. Teachers planning lessons or committees planning curriculum can immediately access the specific standards and areas of content they need for guidance. They can do it from home. Parents also can access the information. No one has to try to remember where their curriculum document is stored and ask for a new copy when they cannot find it. Information on student and school performance is also increasingly on-line. Following are a few examples.

The web-based information is intended for anyone with an interest in the performance of schools in a given locale (region or district) or in the performance of a particular school. Teachers, principals, and parents can evaluate the performance of their school in relation to standards and in relation to the performance of other schools; school board members, civic leaders, and policymakers can evaluate the performance of groups of schools in which they have an interest. The information reveals how well students are achieving in schools, identifies needs for improvement, and depending upon the quality of the measurements, which schools are performing adequately and which schools are not. This creates a more efficient and rational basis for instructional management decision-making, and for allocating rewards, sanctions, and resources aimed at school improvement. Before computer networking and electronic information exchange, performance data on schools was locked exclusively into paper reports that moved slowly through the organization, typically down the organizational hierarchy, from one office to the next. Often it was four or five months after testing before test score reports and other school reports were distributed throughout the organization.

At the school level, administrators would typically have responsibility for disseminating test results among school faculty–a process carried out in a wide variety of ways, with widely varying efficiency, and often involving a lot of photo-copying. The same tasks and difficulties of paper report management described earlier with standards documents also affects the distribution and use of test score. The web and EDI have changed this. Now, routinely, information from statewide testing is available over the web at the same time to everyone–teachers, parents, school principals, guidance counselors, district office curriculum coordinators, personnel supervisors, superintendents, and school board members. Many states and districts also make individual student achievement information available to authorized users. This has created substantially improved access to information for teacher-parent conferencing, for IEP meetings for special education students, and for instructional planning.

Progress Toward SBIA

Education critics are often quick to declare that reforms have failed when dramatic results are not seen after a few years. This perspective reflects an inadequate grasp of the scale and complexity of the education system and that schools' academic influence is shaped greatly by the level of support from home and the values of local communities and wider society. Performance measurement, and information access is significant and should be recognised. The quality of state content and performance standards for curriculum has unquestionably improved, owing to leadership among national curriculum organizations and to the growing stock of experience among dozens of state and district level standards committees. The quality of performance measurement has improved as a result of scholarly advocacy, advances in the psychometric field, and heightened awareness among policymakers and measurement specialists in education agencies. And the revolution in information technology brought to schools networked information systems that have given teachers and administrators much improved access to information on curriculum standards, school performance reports, and student and school profile characteristics.

The standards-based reform and developments in IT. Have these changes at the policy level affected instructional practice in schools? In its ideal formulation, SBIA requires that the planning, instruction, and assessment cycle be integrated among classrooms and grade levels. Standards of achievement should be clearly understood, consistent throughout the school, and guide unit and lesson planning. There should be easy access to student, instructional, and organizational data to monitor performance, to diagnose student needs and problems, and to develop improvement strategies. Undoubtedly, standards-based reform policies have made teachers and principals far more aware of prescribed standards and school performance outcomes today than a decade ago.

We do know that IT can play an important role in facilitating standards-based reform and the implementation of SBIA within schools at the level of instructional practice. Relational data-base management technology and computer-based instructional management systems have gone far toward making SBIA technically feasible. The rapid rise of vendors and software programs for instructional management attests to this. There are a variety of instructional management and information technology systems now available. The goal of these systems is to use computer technology to improve the development and management of lesson plans, student academic records, and information about students' instructional experiences. Reflecting principles of standards-based reform, these instructional management systems almost always have features to link lesson and unit objectives to larger curriculum content and performance standards, whether these standards come from district, state, or national sources. These systems are also designed to manage student achievement records, such as grades and test scores, as well as to record instructional experiences such as lessons and tasks completed, books read, essays written, and the like. While there is very little research specifically on the extent to which instructional management systems are effective in achieving the goals of SBIA within schools and classrooms, available research and theory suggest effectiveness will depend upon several factors:

Leadership and school culture

Values and practices of leaders in the school can either encourage or discourage SBIA. Support for SBIA is created by values and practices such as: norms of collegial conversation that reflect on practice; frequent meetings to examine evidence on instructional practice, staff performance, or student achievement; commitments to professional development and resource support for CRA; and statements, behaviors, and symbols that communicate values of trust, experimentation, and open communication.

School leaders must be experienced, committed, and knowledgeable in order to create these conditions. Often, these conditions do not occur. Instead of trust, teachers or principals may be suspicious that information will be used against them or simply unmotivated to pursue the advantages computers may bring. Such fears are reinforced when test scores are publicly and lead to simplistic media proclamations about "poor teaching and failing schools" or are used inappropriately by uninformed district officials.

Another factor militating against the development of cultures conductive to SBIA is past negative experiences with instructional management or student information technologies. It was not until well in to the 90s that faster CPUs, greater storage capacity, faster connections, better graphical user interfaces and other IT advances made more user-friendly systems possible. During the developmental days of computers in the 80s and even into the 90s untold many schools and districts across the country hastily adopted computer-based instructional management and student information systems sold with promises and attractive presentations, only to find the systems actually complicated, cumbersome, time-consuming, and difficult to use. Frustrating early experiences with computers have left many personnel in schools skeptical about new 'technology solutions' promised by technology advocates outside the school.

There is no getting around the fact that for SBIA to be integrated into instructional practice all or nearly all of the school's faculty and administrators must have a certain level of computer proficiency. While SBIA does not technically require computers, neither does organizing and retrieving information in libraries. Computers and well designed instructional management software are needed to fully realize the potential of SBIA to promote uniform standards within a school, to track student progress through the year and among grades, to report information to users, and to analyze and evaluate results. Despite the ubiquity of computers in schools, teachers and administrators are still predominantly of the pre-computer generation. Many are still reluctant computer users and limited to fairly simple procedures, such as word processing or web-browsing. Compared with prescribed standards of proficiency, the proportion of teachers and principals proficient for more advanced computing uses remains relatively small. With respect to the proficiencies required for data-driven decision-making, for instance, a prominent ULCA education research center describes school decision-makers Information Technology and the Goals of Standards-Based Instruction: as "woefully underprepared to use data [to document results] and for planning and decision-making purposes.

Technical obstacles

Information management systems themselves may have shortcomings that frustrate and impede the goals of users. Administrators and teachers have very little 'down time' during the day and so systems must be designed to provide needed information quickly and easily. While a reasonable level of computer proficiency can be expected, teachers and administrators cannot all be expected to be advanced computer users. The systems must be designed to the maximum extent feasible around the habits and needs of users, rather than users having to adapt inadequately designed systems to the unique conditions in schools and needs of school-based users. Here are a few issues that designers of these systems must consider. All schools have some turnover of students over the course of the school year and many schools have high levels of student turnover. According to one national estimate, one out of six children will attend three schools by the time they are in third grade. It is therefore essential to develop procedures to insure that student databases are current and easy to update. When a new student arrives in a school, the registration information must be entered immediately into the data system and appropriate records up dated. It is a waste of time and discourages reliance on data for planning and decision making if teachers or administrators attempt to use a system and frequently encounter missing or out-of-date information. A closely related issue is linkages between databases. Functionality decreases to the degree that an information management system is unable to pull together current information from different databases. If student demographic and registration information cannot be easily linked with student achievement information and student achievement information cannot be linked with curricular or discipline information, the usefulness of the data declines markedly. It is not enough that the data exist, they must be cross-referenced and easily queried by users.

A third issue concerns the quality of instructional and achievement data. Relatively detailed information is needed for instructional planning. Ideally, SBIA requires at least three types of information: standards-based assessment information, at least once per marking period, from tests and tasks closely aligned with the school's curriculum; state/district achievement test information; and instructional information at the student level related to curriculum objectives. State testing information by itself is inadequate. As Clements observed:

> The decision support systems now under development generally contain the accountability data, because they are the data that are available. These data are considered to be of sufficient quality to warrant widespread use for school and district comparisons and to highlight where effective practice seems to be occurring. While these data may be useful to some decision-makers looking for places where assistance is needed, the data appear to have limited use to teachers and principals seeking to improve what they are doing.

A fourth set of issues concerns the accessibility of the information. Teachers and administrators must be able to use the systems easily. As stated earlier, users should be expected to be proficient with common software programs and commands and basic principles of data analysis and management. At the same time, the systems must be tailored to the needs and proficiency levels of this audience. This means that users must be able to access and query the system from their own computers and produce useful reports as needs arise, without having to struggle with manuals, engage in frequent trial and error, navigate through dozens of screens, and frequently solicit technical consultation. If these standards of ease and functionality cannot be achieved, teachers and principals will of course continue to make instructional and management decisions—only the decisions will be made on the information at hand, however anecdotal, unsystematic, or incomplete it may be.

The most important that will determine the benefits to be derived from the 'next generation' of IT-based instructional management systems for schools. Most schools and districts are still struggling with the challenges of converting existing paper-based data systems to electronic formats and connecting multiple, separate databases to create more integrated, warehoused data management systems. Today in most districts, school-based personnel can access electronically: (a) information on state curriculum content standards and schoolwide profile (b) information on individual students from student records. However, the information of type (a) is in aggregate form and has been compiled by others, while information of type (b) is typically limited to registration, scheduling, and report card information and is difficult to aggregate and analyze. Further, it is typically not the case that all teachers can access information of types (a) or (b) easily from their classrooms on an "as needed" basis. The goal of "next generation" IT systems is to surmount the school-level leadership, personnel proficiency, and technical variables to implement systems that can place at the teachers' fingertips the information necessary to fully realize the vision of SBIA. This can bring standards-based reform more effectively to the classroom level.

7

Virtual Education in World Countries

The globalization of economies has introduced a more sophisticated technology that requires complicated technological competence in each country. Each country has adapted different approaches to this challenge. Higher education (HE) for example, is gradually adjusting to current global socio-economic changes, though tendencies are highly varied. Some countries have high quality performance, while others are near collapse.

Information technology is currently seen as a powerful component in the process of globalization. Computers, the Internet and cheap communication are important in this aspect. Distance is no longer a barrier with satellites transmitting information and images worldwide. Within HE, universities will still play a central role in attempting to respond to the challenges brought by globalization. The role of HE is now shifting from being a reflection of social, cultural and economic relationship to being a determinant of such relationship.

In the USA, the market for commercial learning is expanding and e-Learning is seen as the key to increasing the general knowledge of Americans. People visualize e-Learning as the future trend in the world of learning, whereby all the world's information and knowledge will be accessed via electronic media. Market analysts say the e-Learning network will be worth US$11 billion in about three years.

The global market for e-Learning is growing with virtual universities now found on every continent. In March 1999, the USA based Jones International University (JIU) became the first accredited Internet university, with all the worth of a traditional "bricks and mortar university". Everything here is conducted on the web apart from its administration.It is predicted that during this IT era, virtual universities will benefit the less industrialized countries by producing the very much-needed skilled workers. Countries like Malaysia, India and Kenya are already in this process. Distance education is emerging as an efficient way to bring academic courses and programs to Africa.

The distance education as the use of sophisticated communication technologies to connect geographically dispersed teachers and students. Industrial countries have the best information technology network and in other regions like Latin America and South East Asia, the use of PCs and the Internet has become ordinary. HE in SSA is facing hard times. For example, many students have left for universities abroad and the brain drain phenomenon has developed all over the continent. According to Ben-Barka, "there has developed a situation where universities exist without active research, and are increasingly tilting towards becoming glorified secondary schools". Shola Aboderin, the chief academic officer of the AVU asserts that participation in HE in SSA is between 4 to 6 per cent of the relevant group.

Meanwhile those aged between 15 and 20 have nowhere to go. In Nigeria, for example, only 25 per cent of the qualified students join colleges. Lack of university capacity is identified as the main reason.

The growing knowledge gap experienced in most developing countries was described as "scientific apartheid" by a World Bank official, Ismail Serageldin, at the general conference of the International Association of Universities held in South Africa, at the end of August 2000. He pointed out that between 1980 and 1996, there were sharp inequities in enrolment between the poor and the rich countries, within HE. South Korea was one of the few countries that attempted to bridge the gap with the high-income countries.

Only Taiwan and Hong Kong had more student enrolments in technical subjects than in the OECD countries. Problems in SSA universities include "declining budgets, lack of qualified instructors, and outdated academic programs that fail to meet local needs". Participation in the competitive global economy means that, "this region must produce large numbers of scientifically and technologically literate, innovation-receptive, highly adaptable and problem-solving minded people inclined to lifelong learning". In 1995 the World Bank introduced the concept of 'African Virtual University' to use IT to revolutionize HE in Africa. This ongoing project is seen as a 'lifeline from cyberspace' to the HE system in SSA.

IT in Africa

During the United Nations Economic Commission for Africa (ECA) Conference of Ministers in May 1995,

Resolution 795 entitled "Building Africa's Information Highway" was adopted. This was after the April 1995 Symposium on Telematics for Africa organized by the ECA and the African Networking Initiative.

Around 400 pioneers in electronic communications and delegates from telecommunications authorities in Africa had just met in Addis Ababa, and drafted a communiqué requesting top African government officials to pay attention to the growing global force of IT. They were worried of what it might cost Africa if it was left outside.

The ECA Executive Secretary then appointed a team of 11 experts to draft an action framework to put Africa on the path to use ICT for its development. They met a number of times for one year, and in May 1996 the document was adopted by the ministers and named the African Information Society Initiative (AISI).

AISI was subsequently endorsed by the African Regional Conference on Telecommunications for Development in Abidjan; the OAU Summit of Heads of State and Government; the Information Society and Development Conference; the G-8 meeting and the African Ministers of Communication.

The AISI was conceived in partnership and is currently being implemented in partnership with multilateral, bilateral, non-governmental organizations, research organizations and the private sector. They meet several times annually to discuss major issues concerning ICT in Africa.

The AISI partnership is formed under the Partnership for Information and Communication Technologies in Africa (PICTA), which is an informal group of donors and executing agencies. They are committed to improving information exchange and collaboration around ICT activities in Africa.

The main activities that have been undertaken in partnership since mid-1996 are:

(1) policy awareness campaigns on the Initiative;

(2) organization of policy workshops in over a dozen countries;

(3) organization of workshops on technological, economic and social aspects of connectivity and use of ICT for development;

(4) advisory services on national ICT plans and

(5) projects on democratizing access to the information society

Internet Connectivity in Africa

Only 11 countries in Africa had Internet access at the end of 1996. By September 2000, all the 54 countries and territories had achieved permanent connectivity. Internet access is still largely concentrated in the capital cities though 16 countries have connections (points of presence) in some of the smaller towns.

The total number of computers permanently connected to the Internet moved from 10,000 at the beginning of 1999, to 12,000 in January 2000. It is estimated the figure runs between 25,000-30,000, but because of the technique used in measurement, it is not easy to count hosts not referenced in domain name servers. This means Africa, with 780 million people has almost an equal number of Internet hosts as Latvia .

According to a recent study by the ECA, figures for the dialup subscriber accounts to Internet Service Providers (ISPs) are estimated at over 1 million subscribers in Africa. About 200,000 are in North Africa, 650,000 in South Africa and 150,000 in the remaining 50 countries. It is estimated that Africa currently has a total of around 3 million users, with approximately 1 million outside of South Africa.

There is 1 Internet user for every 250 people in Africa "compared to a world average of about one user for every 35 people, and a North American and European average of about one in every 3 people". It is reported that although no studies have been made in Africa to determine the number of rural and urban users, those in the cities and towns greatly surpass rural Internet users. "On a sub-regional basis, Southern and North Africa are the most advanced regions in terms of their use of ICTs, followed by East and West Africa with Central Africa lagging furthest behind". Because of their advanced economies and better infrastructure, these countries have larger Internet user populations. It currently costs about US$ 50 per month to use a local dialup account for 5 hours in Africa.

ISP charges greatly differ between US$ 10- US$ 100 per month. This is so because of market developments and the varying tariff policies of the telecom operators. The different national policies on "private wireless data services and on access to international telecommunications bandwith" add to the variation. There is a rapid growth of cyber cafés and other types of public Internet access like adding PCs to community phone shops, clinics and schools.

Public telecom operators have also moved into the Internet services market very rapidly in most African countries. In some countries these operators are the main international link providers while the national Internet services are left for private providers. It is still a major problem to deliver web pages over the Internet due to high international tariffs and less circuit capacity in many countries.

Therefore a large number of African Internet sites are hosted on servers in Europe or the USA. ECA notes that on the average, Africa has one incoming and one outgoing email everyday, mostly with persons outside the continent. The ECA survey of the Internet users realized that most users were male: 86 per cent in Ethiopia, 83 percent in Senegal and 64 per cent in Zambia. The majority was well educated: 87 percent of users in Zambia and 98 per cent in Ethiopia had a university degree.

All over Africa, email users report that they now witness an increase in efficiency and reduced communication costs, though the e-mail is basically used in contacting people in other regions. However, the Web is still generally under-utilized. The ECA survey reported that 40 percent of Zambian users had carried out literature searches on the Web.

Universities were at the forefront in initiating Internet developments in Africa and most of them do provide e-mail services. Nevertheless, at the beginning of 1999, only 20 countries had universities with full Internet connectivity. Full Internet access is often restricted to staff, due to the limited resources and high costs of computer facilities and bandwidth. The general student body usually has no access apart from the post-graduates.

The African web-space is also rapidly growing with many institutions being hosted on servers locally or internationally. Many organizations have web sites with basic descriptive and contact information. Very few use the Web for their activities mainly "because of the limited numbers that access the Internet, the limited skills available for digitizing and coding pages and the high costs of local web hosting".

The ECA survey realized that there were a few official general government web sites. Nothing indicated that governments are using the Internet for existing administrative purposes. Sectors involved in tourism and foreign investment use the web for developing an international market presence. It was also noted that although most ministries and research centers have access to email, quite a few have a web site. The survey found that government employees made up only 1 percent of users in Ethiopia and only 6 percent in Zambia.

The advanced profile on the Web by the French speaking countries and greater institutional connectivity compared to the non-French speaking countries. The various Francophone support agencies and the French and Canadian governments highly support them. They are also concerned about the dominance of English on the Internet.

The African Virtual University

The term 'African Virtual University' (AVU) was first introduced in 1995 by the World Bank, as a concept to define the partnership between some institutions of higher learning in sub-Saharan Africa, and those in the

United States and Europe. The World Bank is attempting through this project, to widely use the power of information technologies to improve access to the highly needed educational resources in SSA.

The World Bank Education Sector has pledged to work hard to bring SSA into the global education picture. It is a welcoming idea that this organization has accepted to change its overpowering attitude applied here for many years, and will instead 'listen and partner', as a new approach. The World Bank Africa Region approved the AVU as a regional initiative in August 1995. To initiate preparation activities for this goal, a budget of US$ 212,000 was allocated during the fiscal year (FY) 96.

The Information for Development Program (INFODEV) at the World Bank approved a grant to the amount of US$ 250,000 for paying the consultants assisting with the preparations. INFODEV supports innovative projects that use IT to address development projects. A further grant of US$ 365,000 was approved by the United States Trade Development Agency (USTDA) to US consultants to design and develop the network infrastructure.

During the FY 96, a lot was learnt about technology-based distance education worldwide by consulting expertise in the field. It was also important to design, develop and market the concept of AVU to key implementation partners like African universities, universities with established technology-based distance education programs in the West, technical service providers, etc.

In early 1996, a team of consultants set to define an initial technical network topology comprising a satellite video-instructional program, an academic curriculum overview for an undergraduate degree program in science, engineering and nursing studies, a digital library planning document, and an administrative infrastructure needs. These were carried out during the FYs 96 and 97. Field visits were conducted in a number of African universities, which indicated willingness to team up with the World Bank in the implementation of a pilot operation to test the concept.

In February 1997, two well-attended workshops to demonstrate and familiarize participants with the network design and operating procedures were held in Addis Ababa for the English speaking universities. In April 1997, one was held in Dakar for the French speaking universities. African universities thereafter confirmed their participation in the AVU. They then started putting in place the human resource infrastructure to run the AVU at their respective campuses.

The Africa Region granted resources to finance the acquisition and installation of satellite receiving terminal equipment in six English-speaking countries. Training programs for staff involved in the implementation of the AVU at each campus were initiated, and subscriptions were made to academic journals in digital formats. The financing of receiving site terminals in French speaking countries was also made possible through existing education projects.

The first AVU courses were delivered to English-speaking countries in July 1997. Course programming for Francophone learning centers started in March 1999. INFODEV has so far spent US$ 1 million on the project.

The prototype service phase started in 1997 to test the assumptions and models of the project, and to establish the operating structure of the university. The initial operations phase that started in 1998, to offer complete degree programs and a complete set of other products and services.

During the final operations phase, partner African institutions will start offering locally prepared programs and degrees in October 2001. It is hoped that within four years of operations, the AVU will be will be self-financing. The prototype and initial operations phases have been sponsored by the World Bank, the private sector and government agencies in Africa and abroad.

AVU's mission is to bridge the digital divide and knowledge gap between Africa and the rest of the world by dramatically increasing access to global educational resources throughout Africa. This will be achieved through the integration of satellite and Internet technologies to allow for cost-effective and efficient delivery of educational programs throughout sub-Saharan Africa and to access educational resources globally as well as the best in sub-Saharan Africa.

The AVU currently works with 25 partner institutions in 15 countries and plans to reach more countries in Africa, undergraduate students, faculty and professionals. This will be achieved through learning centers in public universities, private franchises (private universities or training centers); and on-site professional learning centers housed in corporations and non-governmental organizations (NGOs) AVU courses are delivered through an integration of satellite and Internet technologies, allowing quality educational content from all parts of the world at affordable costs.

This is important considering the technological and infrastructure limitations currently existing in Africa: "To ensure pedagogical effectiveness, AVU places high premium on interactivity and local learner support". Renowned professors worldwide deliver courses from a studio-classroom then are transmitted to AVU's central uplink facilities in Clarksburg, Maryland (USA). These are then beamed by satellite to its learning centers across Africa, which are equipped with inexpensive satellite dishes that receive the signal.

A studio should have at least two phone lines, a fax and a computer with Internet connection to conduct the question and answer section of the session. The University of Massachusetts (USA), the New Jersey Institute of Technology (USA) and the University College Galway (Ireland) are some of the participating institutions (ibid.).

A normal AVU classroom has between 25-30 students, who sit at their desks watching the broadcast on large screen projectors, television or computer monitors. "During the sessions, students have the chance for real-time interaction with the instructor using phone lines, e-mail or fax.

For example, a student in Rwanda can ask a professor in Togo or Paris questions that can be heard and responded to by students in Benin and Senegal". These questions can be answered during or after the broadcast. Courses are offered in both English and French. In future, courses will also be offered in Portuguese. Each AVU learning center has an on-site moderator available to guide the students through the materials, and act as liaison with course instructors.

AVU future plans include upgrading its technology to provide for a two-way video and audio, and a fast Internet connectivity, to increase the chances of web-based course delivery. The AVU is more concerned with the quality of materials delivered than the technology it uses. One goal of AVU is to continually strive "to find innovative, improved and pragmatic ways to deliver quality education to the students of sub-Saharan Africa".

The main areas of knowledge catered to by AVU are those within economic development, currently not provided by institutions of higher learning. During the pilot phase, certificate-based courses have been offered in science, engineering and technology, management and health programs.

From October 2001, AVU will offer degree programs in electrical and computer engineering and computer science. An Internet-based digital library of journals, academic studies and textbooks, is available at AVU for both students and teachers. This web-based resource offers research materials unavailable in local libraries. To register at AVU, one can call, fax or e-mail an AVU learning center stating what course she/he wishes to take. Course prices differ depending on the course offered.

Academic courses target the undergraduate and pre-university level. Basic and more advanced courses in computer, business, and professional development seminars, target both professors and students. English is offered as a second language for the Francophone countries, while remedial English for the Anglophone countries. An institution does not have to be the course owner.

Videotapes can be licensed from the producer, although the institution should provide the instructor, studio facilities and uplink. To transmit the live broadcasts, AVU seeks institutions having studio facilities and videoconferencing capabilities and/or satellite uplink capacity. There are usually 5-8 live sessions of 1 hour 30 minutes to I hour 45 minutes. Courses are often conducted between 6.00 a.m. and 4.00 p.m. due to the vast time differences between the learning centers.

Course materials and videos are previewed by AVU and after a decision has been reached, the producer/ institution submits an estimate. All course proposals have to be relevant to the needs and standards of AVU. Faculty members also provide syllabi, course notes, tests and exams, recommended reading and lists of Web resources as required.

AVU learning centers can be established at any place with a prospective market for learning, and not necessarily on university campuses. A learning center can therefore be established and managed privately in urban areas or in areas with high demand for educational training. For those who wish to purchase necessary equipment to start up an AVU learning center, Infotel Systems (AVU equipment suppliers) can provide necessary quotations.

The demand for AVU's courses is high, aiming at all types of students and professionals. At KU, participating students are already paying fees. However, challenges may arise at the final operations phase, when AVU is expected to be self-reliant. Most SSA countries have in the past proved to be inefficient in applying effective market policies for cost recovery.

In addition to this, given the unfavorable macro-economic circumstances here, it may be difficult to achieve the 'customer-driven' objective. Most students in traditional universities often have problems with sustaining their education privately. Equity of participation may not be achieved if course prices are not affordable to all.

Virtual universities are a welcome idea especially with the increasing quest for more knowledge. However, many view it as an extension of the old 'Western hegemony' coming in another form. The virtual university as "a reality with implications for higher education and internationalization". The concept of AVU but fears that "the greater danger may lie in AVU's potential for accelerating the growing intellectual hegemony of the United States and Europe through domination of the content of information and communications technology on which the AVU is based", the forces of globalization and IT may not offer solutions to Africa's problems at the micro-level.

Within education, "digitalized learning may be quick in spreading and exchanging views, but it lacks that intimacy between scholars found in traditional learning". The goal of this new type of knowledge is to allow as much access as possible to people. According to Taylor, the British Computer Society feels that "Schools of the future are likely to be framed (or limited) by 'walls of the mind' rather than by organizational or building structures". The implication here is that students may have to reconfigure their minds to suit the technology. "New technologies are introduced to the educational process with scant prior evidence of their pedagogical benefits, and with the axiomatic threat that failure to adopt them, means you will be left further behind in the IT race to no one knows where".

He says, "The technology-sponsored devaluation of education is underwritten and reinforced by a wider cultural commitment to its McDonaldization". Students are turning into customers with rights and no responsibilities. Previously logical courses have been replaced with "extra-value" meal equivalents: stand alone modules. "Lateral associations, de-contextualized information and hypertext links are slowly replacing deep knowledge acquired from wide reading and long reflection".

Taylor fears that inappropriate technology is affecting education. For example, the Internet does not allow for the process of book professional book reviews and critique before reaching students. He concludes that although the Internet has a wealth of information, it is seldom that its weaknesses are mentioned.

In a study carried out by Rosenberg on IT and resource sharing problems within selected SSA university libraries, she realized that the introduction of new technologies was an additional cost burden. It was expensive to maintain and update both the hardware and software. Databases were costly because the technology and quality of PCs changed quite fast. The University of Zimbabwe for example, had no computer service contracts, meaning that maintenance was non-existent.

The service contract on the library hardware cost US$ 28,000 per annum at the University of Botswana, while the software cost US$ 18,000 per annum without the cost of spares and updates. This was definitely more than what most libraries spent on books and journals. This could also mean that they had to either look for emergency funds, or close the services. In Rosenberg's study, "the first priority was to have books in multiple copies, more journals, newer books and more space". Because of the cost of computers and problems of document delivery, IT cannot reduce the need for books and journals.

Research findings published in the London based Library Management journal in June 2000 appealed for more thorough in-service training for librarians in the public universities of Kenya. "Service delivery at these universities was hindered due to incompetence, poor remuneration, lack of motivation and teamwork". This research recommended that university librarians should turn to the World Bank-funded AVU to ensure access to diversified materials. Kenyan universities were urged to review their operations as the era of information technology engenders itself. "Indeed, if they do not adopt online searches, cataloguing and database design, public university libraries may lose many users to other information centers that utilize services such as Internet searches".

Since IT resources are lacking in most SSA university libraries, it is likely that skills gained from the AVU may be lost since they cannot be shared. Maintenance of equipment, wherever available, is also in question. In general, IT does not provide a solution to the decline of the African university library.

Inadequate computer literacy and facilities amongst academics in SSA are additional problems in disseminating knowledge via the Internet. The use of information on the World Wide Web requires the user to have access to the vital technical equipment and infrastructure and also to understand how to apply the technology. It will therefore take time to close the digital divide. The lack of sound infrastructure only limits the spread of knowledge even for those with computer literacy. The IT environment changes quite fast, demanding continuous training.

Since most institutions lack strong IT policies, they need to draft guidelines to be used in developing strategic IT plans.

"The economic environment all over Africa is changing as market economies become predominant. Government funding for HE is therefore not automatic". Both political and financial skills are needed to exploit this new environment. There is a challenge for HE to justify its existence and importance to, the academic process. For HE in SSA to survive, it must be open to accountability, continual evaluation of decisions rendered, income earned and results achieved. There must be better communication channels between financiers and partners.

Virtual Education in China

The educational level of the Chinese population is still very low. According to the 1995 Sample Census, people who had received college education accounted for only about 2 percent of the total population, which is very low compared with other countries. The restructuring in education during the 1990s has been characterized by continued decentralization of finance and administration and control in general, growing impact of market mechanisms, increased pressure for efficiency and effectiveness, privatization, and more individualization.

In the era of globalization, higher education in China is facing the challenges of 'virtualization' and e-Learning to meet the requirements of mass education at all levels.

Virtual higher education can be seen as a new generation of distance learning in China from the perspective of the principles, methods and instrumental operation of educational technology.

Distance education has experienced three generations of development from the perspectives of educational technology employed to provide distance-learning courses: the modes of delivery of the first generation were mainly printed material, radio, and television; in the second generation multiple modern technologies were applied, such as, besides, computers, audiocassettes, television, videocassettes, fax, and printed material; the third generation added e-mail, chat sessions, bulletin boards, computer networks, CDs, the Internet, audio conferencing, videocon-ferencing, and satellite transmission.

The general chronology of the development of distance education in China can also be summarized in three stages, i.e.

(1) correspondence education,

(2) radio-visual education, and

(3) modern distance education based on digital techniques, the Internet, and multiple information systems.

The present development of virtual higher education has its roots in the 'traditional' distance education. There are three-stage development of traditional distance education in China from its traditional mode to modern ICT and Internet based virtual education and e-Learning.

Distance education in China can thus be traced back to the provision of correspondence courses in the early 50s. The Evening College in the National People's University set up a correspondence education curriculum in 1953. About 2,500 students were enrolled, majoring in finance and economics. This was the first effort at correspondence education after the founding of the People's Republic in 1949.

After 1953, correspondence education departments were set up one after another in a number of major universities in Beijing, Shanghai, and the Northeast region. By 1957, 58 institutions of higher education ran correspondence courses with a total enrollment of 35,000 students. These institutions included universities and colleges of science and engineering, liberal arts, agriculture, forestry, teacher's training, finance and economics, political science and law.

The School of Agriculture of Jinling University had conducted the first audiovisual education program in China already in the 1920s. Slides and films were used with oral explanations recorded on phonograph to publicize the scientific methods for cotton planting.

Audiovisual education was then developed in various schools at all levels after 1949. Radio and television universities were established in Beijing, Shanghai, and Shenyang in 1960. The educational television system was started in the early 1960s in Beijing and the first television set was produced by 'New China' in 1962. During the anti-academic and anti-intellectual "cultural revolution", they were suspended and did not restart again until at the end of the 1970s.

In 1978, the State Council approved the setting up of the Central Radio and Television University (CRTVU) and the Central Audio-Visual Center in China. Later, radio and television universities and audiovisual centres were restored or established in twenty-eight provinces, autonomous regions, and municipalities. The Television

University of Shanghai was reopened during this period, covering large areas and supplying great educational contents.

The China Educational Television Station was established in 1986 and provincial education television stations were set up soon after in the provinces and cities of Liaoning, Jilin, Shanghai, Jiangsu, Fujian, Jiangxi, Ningxia, Xinjiang and other regions. The Central Radio and Television University, in China known as 'Dianda', is a network comprising a central open university in Beijing and forty-three open universities in each province and major municipalities in China.

Now, it is not only the largest higher education institution in China, but also in the world. The main task of the CRTVU is to provide professional, vocational and continuing education for adults. It is an extremely decentralized system, largely confined to urban areas, with local centres being responsible for student administration. The central administration in Beijing has no individual records.

In 1987, the Central Radio and Television University had its programs produced, transmitted and financed by the Ministry of Radio Cinema and Television. The State Education Commission, which is now The Ministry of Education, developed its curriculum and distributed its printed support materials.

The curriculum included both basic, general-purpose courses in science and technology and more specialized courses. Programs with English-language instruction were particularly popular. Many students studying in the Central Radio and Television University are recent graduates from upper secondary schools whose scores are just below the cutoff points for admission to conventional colleges and universities. There are full-time students, part-time students, and spare-time students who study after work.

Students, whose work units grant them permission to study at a television university, are paid their normal wages; expenses for most of their books and other educational materials are paid for by the state. A typical Central Radio and Television University student spends up to six hours a day over a three-year period watching lectures on videotapes produced by some of the best teachers in China.

Students who pass final examinations are given certificates entitling them to the same level of remuneration as graduates of regular, full-time colleges and universities. The state provides certain allowances to students awaiting jobs during their training period.

Three-year and two-year degrees are awarded. The three-year program is designed primarily for those full-time students who must finish their study in three years. The two-year program is designed for full time students of the Humanities who are either working adults or recent upper-secondary-school graduates. The whole delivery system has a hierarchical structure.

At the national, central level, the Ministry of Education has established the China Education Television Station (CETV), which is responsible for editing and broadcasting education programs. Cooperating with the Ministry of Post and Telecommunications, CETV operates an earth station to up-link programs into INTELSAT V and CHINASAT. At the local level of the delivery system, TV relay stations are built in big cities and population centres.

People can receive programs using TV sets in the workplace and at home. Because of the country's varied topography with different reception conditions, it is more efficient to build many TV relay stations with small transmitting power rather than fewer stations with great power. TV Receiving Only (TVRO) earth stations are widely used in small towns, villages, organizations and schools. Usually, these stations are equipped with videocassette recorders. Programs are recorded for later viewing or for delivery to learning centres.

Print materials, including textbooks, reference books, and study guides, are combined with videotapes to form a learning package. Every day, the two channels broadcast a total of thirty one hours. Provincial education stations that broadcast their own programs share the rest of the broadcast day. In the 1990s, about 20 million people viewed educationai programs or took courses either at home or in 30,000 learning centres. During the Tenth Five-Year Plan period, one more Satellite TV channel will be dedicated to primary and secondary students. More TV relay stations will be established so that 70 percent of the areas in all countries will be covered.

In 1986, the National People's Congress of China decided to develop a distance education system based on satellite transmission. The project was planned in three phases:

In the first phase, leasing and purchasing transponders from INTELSAT carried out a series of pilot programs for distance education, and a ground network was built.

In the second phase, China's communication satellite was made and launched. This satellite is complemented by the leased and purchased transponders. A second channel is available for delivering educational programs.

In the third phase, a Chinese-made communication satellite with twenty-four transponders will be launched to form the domestic satellite communication system. Additional channels will be devoted to distance education.

The Satellite Education Channel 1 started broadcasting programs on October 1, 1986. The China Education Television (CETV) was established in 1987 and the second and third channels followed up in 1988 and 1994 responsible for transmitting educational programs.

The contents include degree education of radio and television universities, continuing education for teachers and principals, secondary specialties and vocational education, and practical-skills training courses for peasants. Channel 1 broadcasts educational news and comprehensive educational programs. Channel 2, which focuses on the courses of CRTVU, and Channel 3, which is mainly responsible for the popularization of the nine-year compulsory education, are jointly run by the Ministry of Education and the government of the Shandong province. The Beijing Educational Channel, which covers the whole Beijing area, was established by CETV in October 1996.

The network of distance higher learning made great strides in the 1980s. Enrollment of degree students amounted to more than 1.73 million, while graduates have totaled over 1.18 million since 1982. Additionally, millions of single-course and post-tertiary continuing education students have been served.

The total number of Television University degree graduates between 1982 and 1989 was 40 percent of conventional universities and colleges in the same period of time throughout China. In 1986, the number of graduates majoring in economic management amounted to more than 200,000, which was 1.2 times the number of those who had graduated from conventional universities and colleges over the 39 years since the founding of the People's Republic of China in 1949.

At present, the radio and television education system consists of the CRTVU, 44 provincial radio and television universities (RTVUs), 831 municipal-level radio and television universities and 1699 county-level branches. A large number of correspondence divisions affiliated to regular tertiary and specialized secondary institutions. In addition, 152 RTV specialized secondary schools are being set up. There are over 700 educational television stations throughout the country.

According to the 1997 statistics, the total accumulated number of graduates of the three-year radio and television colleges was more than 2.3 million and the total enrollment was over 700,000.

The Case of The Agricultural Broadcasting School

There are 900 million people living in rural areas in China. They are scattered over the vast countryside. Many farmers have never left their native town, nor have they had access to secondary or higher education. It is impossible to improve their scientific and educational qualification through solely traditional schooling.

The Agricultural Broadcasting School (ABS) was established in 1980 by the joint efforts of the Ministry of

Agriculture, the Ministry of Education and some other departments. The ABS provides distance education to farmers by means of broadcasting, TV, audio and video recordings, VCDs and a computer network. It has helped accelerate the cultivation of qualified agricultural personnel and the spread of science and technology.

The ABS now has 46,000 full-time and part-time teaching and administrative staff. It comprises a central school, about 40 province-level schools, more than 300 prefecture-level schools, more than two thousand county-level schools and more than twenty thousand teaching classes in towns and townships. The ABS offers more than 100 specialties and has published many textbooks and recorded audio and video teaching programs.

By 1999, the ABS had trained 3 million secondary and higher special technical and managerial personnel. Nearly two and half million farmers had received one-year primary education and nearly a hundred million farmers had participated in organized training of applied techniques.

Modern Distance Education

Modern distance education is a new type of education that has come into being with the development of the modern information technology, digital techniques, Internet, multimedia technology, etc. It is a major means to build up a lifelong learning system meeting the needs of people living in an era of knowledge economy.

The "Modern Distance Education Project" implemented on the basis of existing distance education facilities and making full use of modern information technology is expected effectively to take full advantage of available educational resources. But in view of the shortage of such resources, this is also a strategic step to extend access to education for the large population of the country.

The Action Scheme for Invigorating Education towards the 21st Century regarded modern distance education as one of the key projects in China. The target of the project is to set up initially a modern distance education network, to construct a series of backbone courses, and to search for a teaching and administration pattern suitable for China's modern distance education through three years of efforts. In view of the disparities of social and economic development among regions, the promotion of modern distance.education has been divided into three levels:

(1) the popularization and utilization of education technology with multimedia computer skills as its core;
(2) the popularization and application of network to improve the teaching quality; and
(3) the opening of a modern cyber education system to construct and provide large quantities of network resources and meet the increasing needs of lifelong education in society.

A network with complete structures will exist by 2010 to provide opportunities of life-long education for the public with modern distance education and education suitable for rural and outlying districts.

In order to search for the proper pattern of modern distance education, Qinghua University, Beijing University of Post and Telecommunication, Zhejiang

University and Hunan University were designated as the key experimental universities and the relevant experiments are being carried out at present.

A recent structure and system that will play a great role in distance education in China is CERNET, which is a government-sponsored nationwide academic computer network to support the basic education and research environment in the country. Under the direction of the Ministry of Education, ten universities have formed a national Internet backbone to link up eight major regions in China.

Today, CERNET connects 100 universities and some middle schools to each other and to the Internet. Located at Qinghua University in Beijing, the CERNET National Network Center is responsible for the construction, operation and management of CERNET.

Playing important roles in CERNET, regional network centres are responsible for the operation and management of regional networks, as well as the admission of institutions and users within their domains into CERNET. Regional network centres also provide technical support to the individual universities. Distributed among ten universities in eight cities, the regional network centres and the main nodes function as bridges between the campus networks and CERNET.

China has joined more and more international organizations and has made great efforts to cooperate in all areas with the UN and the rest of the world and has furthermore been very active in pushing forward the North-South Dialogue and South-South cooperation. There has also been a gradual expansion of international cooperation and exchange in education with the implementation of the policy of opening to the outside world.

The Internet is playing an important role in China's interaction with the rest of the world. A great number of Chinese media units have been connected with Internet. These units include the China Net Information Center (CIC), People's Daily, Xinhua News Agency, Beijing Review, China Daily and China Central Television, etc.

With the development of the Internet, the Chinese media is placing much stress on publicizing the country's culture, reform and the opening up through the new communications medium. It has become very popular with users for its convenience and timeliness, as well as its interchangeable Chinese and foreign language versions.

The usage of the Internet in China has been expanded enormously during the last few years. There were about 50,000 Internet users in 1995 (The Economist, 2000). By the end of 2000, this number reached to 22.5 million, an increase by 450 times.

Since 1997, China Internet Network Information Center (CNNIC), in cooperation with other institutions, has been conducting surveys on the development of Internet in China. The latest "Semiannual Survey Report on the Development of China's Internet" was published in July 2000. According to the report, there were 6.5 million computer hosts and 16.9 million Internet users in China in July 2000, compared with 0.54 million computer hosts and 1.175 million Internet users in July 1998.

.The expansion of Internet usage in China in the last three years of the last century is shown in Table 1. As to gender and age distribution of the Internet users, females have increased during the last two years. Male users still maintain their dominance, 75 percent of the total.

Table: 1 Internet Expansion

Time	Computer hosts	Internet users	No. of Websites
July 1998	542 000	1 175 000	3 700
July 1999	1 460 000	4 000 000	9 906
July 2000	6 500 000	16 900 000	27 289
Decem2000*	8 920 000	22 500 000	265 405

Around 90 percent of the Internet users are under 35 years. Generally speaking, most Internet users are well educated. Those who have attained BA or MA degree account for about sixty percent of the total while the portion of two-three years college students is increasing yearly. The educational background is summarized in Table 2.

Table 2: Educational Background of Internet Users in Percent

Time	2-3 year college	Bachelor degree	Master degree or higher
July 1998	34	50	9
July 1999	39	48	11
July 2000	46	46	6

The implementation of online recruitment is an important reform of higher education in China. In 1999, nine provinces carried out experiments on online recruitment. Such recruitment has been found to make the selection procedure more efficient and fair. By the year 2000, more than half of the provinces and more than half of higher education institutions were expected to practice online recruitment on an experimental basis, and more than half of the new university students would be selected through online recruitment. China's top legislative body recently endorsed a resolution on maintaining security of computer networks, checking on unlawful online activities and helping boost the fledging IT sector in China. According to the resolution, some actions are regarded as criminal offence. For example, to enter networks concerned with national security; to create and spread computer viruses and to interrupt computer networks or communication services; to spread rumors and slanders or publicize harmful information on Internet; to stir up ethnic hatred and discrimination, and sabotage national unity through Internet; to organize a cult organization; to infringe upon other people's intellectual property; etc. The resolution is believed to play a positive role in protecting the rights of citizens and corporations on the network.

It shows that distance education in China has deep roots far back in the last century. But the coverage has been constrained by the low technological level and the general poverty of the country. It is also clear that the new economic, political and educational strategies adopted in the 1980s and 1990s have led to rapid development and expansion of distance education. Still, even when a modern economy as well as international contacts and exchange were developing and modern ICT and Internet access were available, China was rather late compared to many other countries in the world in entering the stage of Internet based virtual education and e-Learning. The indications are that the main reasons for this were political. The Chinese leadership feared than unrestricted Internet access would open up for unwanted influences, ideas and contacts. However, with the development of the market economy and the expanding international trade and the acceptance of the new information and communication technologies, the applications of ICT both in education and society at large were extremely rapid in the last years of the 1990s. The use of computers and the Internet is now expanding at a very high speed in all sectors of society.

Bibliography

Ackermann, E., *Tools for Teaching: The World Wide Web and a Web Browser*, 1996.

Bricken, M. and Byrne, C. M., "Summer children in virtual reality: a pilot study on educational applications of virtual reality technology", In Wexelblat, A (ed.) *Virtual reality: Applications and Explorations*. Academic, Boston, 1993.

Burdea, Grigore and Coiffet, Phillippe, *Virtual Reality Technology*, Wiley-Interscience Publication, 1994.

Cromby, J., Standen, P. and Brown, D., "Using Virtual Reality in Special Education", *VR in the Schools*, 1, 3, 14, 1995.

Dede, C. J., "The Future of Multimedia: Bridging to Virtual Worlds, *Educational Technology*, 1992.

Ferrington, G. and Loge, K., "Virtual Reality: A New Learning Environment", *The Computing Teacher*, 1992.

Heim, M., *Virtual Realism*, New York: Oxford University Press, 1998.

Hiltz, R. S., *The Virtual Classroom*, Norwood, NJ: Ablex, 1995.

Jorn D., Hill Duin A. and Wahlstrom B., 'Designing and Managing Virtual Learning Communities' *IEEE Transactions of Professional Communication*. 39(4), 1996.

Kelly, R. V., The end of cognitive Bulimia, *Virtual Reality Special Report*, 3, 1, 38-50, 1996.

Loeffler, Carl E. and Anderson, Tim, (ed.), *The Virtual Reality Casebook*. Van Nostrand Reinhold, 1994.

Maddox, C. C., *The World Wide Web and School Culture: Are they Compatible?*, in D. L. Johnson, C. D. Maddux, and L. Lieu, (eds.), *Using Technology in the Classroom*, New York: The Haworth Press, 1997.

Newby, G., "Virtual reality", In Williams, M. E. (ed.), *Annual Review of Information Science and Technology*, 1993.

Osberg, K. M., "Virtual Reality and Education: Where Imagination and Experience Meet", *VR in the Schools*, 1995.

Pantelidis, V. S., "Virtual Reality in the Classroom", *Educational Technology*, 1993.

Penny. S., "Virtual Body Building", *Media Information*, Australia no. 69, 1993.

Pimentel, Ken and Teixeira, Kevin, *Virtual Reality: Through the New Looking Glass*, Second Edition. Mc Graw-Hill, Inc., 1995.

Tiffy J., "The Search for the Virtual Class", *The Virtual University Symposium: A report,* D. Baird (ed.) UltiBASE http://ultibase.rmit.edu.au/Articles/maher1.html, 1996.

Winn, W. and Bricken, W., "Designing Virtual worlds for Use in Mathematics Education: The example of Experiential Algebra, *Educational Technology*, 1992.

Index